INTERNATIONAL FOLK PLAYS

A scene from *The Wandering Dragon* by Lily T'ang. Lee
Mu, the Mother, "seated in her carriage," instructs her
daughters, Lee Fong Fong and Lee Shiao Fong, to look
after the Inn while she is away.

INTERNATIONAL FOLK PLAYS

EDITED
with an Introduction by
SAMUEL SELDEN

Chapel Hill
THE UNIVERSITY OF NORTH CAROLINA PRESS

A royalty fee is required for each performance of any of these plays either by amateurs or by professionals. Special arrangements must be made for broadcasting.

The amateur acting rights, and the radio and television rights, to these plays are controlled by Samuel French, 25 West 45th Street, New York, N. Y., or 7623 Sunset Blvd., Hollywood 46, Calif., or 480-486 University Avenue, Toronto, Canada, to whom application should be made for production.

TO THE MEMORY OF

FREDERICK HENRY KOCH

WHOSE SPIRIT MOVES

THROUGH THESE PAGES

INTRODUCTION

On the evening of March 14, 1919, at the University of North Carolina, the newly-founded Carolina Playmakers presented two one-act plays written by students in Professor Frederick Koch's course in playwriting. The plays were *When Witches Ride*, a dramatization of a Northhampton County folk superstition, by Elizabeth Lay, later Mrs. Paul Green; and *The Return of Buck Gavin*, about a Western Carolina mountain outlaw, by Thomas Wolfe. Across the top of the playbill for that performance was printed "ORIGINAL FOLK PLAYS." As far as we know, this was the first time the term "folk play" had been used in the American Theatre. That was thirty years ago; since then the term has come into fairly common use, not only in the South, but elsewhere.

Professor Koch explained his concept of folk drama in the September, 1939, issue of *The Carolina Play-Book*. "The term folk drama, as we use it," he said, "has nothing to do with the folk play of medieval times (often attributed by scholars to communal authorship) which took the form of Christmas pantomimes by village mummers, jigs, sword dances, festivals, and other community celebrations. More recently it has been applied to the peasant plays of the Irish Renaissance written by a single author dealing consciously with the folkways of our less sophisticated people living simple lives apart from the present-day, complex social order. With us too the plays deal with folk subject matter, with legends, superstitions, cus-

vii

toms, environmental differences, and the vernacular of
the common people. For the most part they are realistic
and human; sometimes they are imaginative and poetic.
... The term 'folk' ... applies to that form of drama
which is earth-rooted in the life of our common human-
ity." Professor Koch cited as examples of the modern folk
play Eugene O'Neill's *Beyond the Horizon* and *The
Hairy Ape*, Marc Connelly's *Green Pastures*, and Thorn-
ton Wilder's *Our Town*, and as representatives of the
opposite type Noel Coward's sophisticated parlor come-
dies and Bernard Shaw's dialectic pieces. At no time did
Professor Koch seek to belittle such dramatists as Coward
and Shaw, both of whom he admired; he merely stated
that their purposes are different.

The idea of folk drama has evolved somewhat since the
early days. The first plays were reportorial in nature,
occupied chiefly with the shadowed side of life among
underprivileged rural people—Negroes, mountaineers,
fishermen, tenant farmers. (The use of legends and superstitions was incidental.) The characters were poor and
unhappy. The picturization of them was dark—sometimes very dark indeed! In the years that have passed the
playwrights have come to see their folk subjects from
new angles. Their perspective has widened. They have
grown more interested in the whole man, rather than
in just the colorful features of his external personality.

The folk play today is still "earth-rooted," but no
longer is it necessarily tragic, and the people in it do not
come from any particular class or locality. Many of the
best plays written at Carolina since 1919 have had their
settings in towns and cities. Every student author who
has an ambition to be a "folk dramatist" is encouraged
to deal honestly and simply with what he knows best. If
his background is Jonesville, he writes about the kind of
people he has walked and talked with there. If his back-

ground is New York City, he writes about that. If the place of his upbringing is Alaska, he writes about that, resisting all temptations to dramatize something in Louisiana which he has never seen.

Folk plays now are composed in every kind of mood, light or dark, gay or profound, and in every style from realism to fantasy. The term "folk" covers for us a wide range of subject matter and treatment. The one unalterable requisite of a folk play is that it be concerned principally not with smartness, wittiness, or intellectual exercise, but rather with some fundamental hunger common to all men—a hunger for bread, shelter, affection, elemental beauty, or a little light to illuminate the mind.

INTERNATIONAL FOLK PLAYS

The nine plays in this collection are folk dramas, written by Dramatic Art students at the University of North Carolina. The scenes here are not domestic, however, but foreign. These are international folk plays. They are one indication of the way the original concept has grown. The plays are folk dramas, we say, because the scenes are real, the characters are earthy, and their desires are common. Even the Emperor in *The Wandering Dragon* belongs, for he is viewed by the author, not through the eyes of his courtiers, but through the lowlier eyes of his subjects among whom he travels. And he solves the momentous problem of finding for himself a suitable imperial consort by choosing a lovely, but simple, country girl!

NORWAY: *Home-Longing*

Gerd Bernhart, author of the first play, was born in the oldest city of Norway, Tönsberg. This is the place her heroine, Karen, remembers lovingly, dreaming of it through the long nights in her little village in the north. When Miss Bernhart was still very young she came with her parents to the United States and made her home at Sioux Falls, South Dakota, where she grew up. When she was twenty years old, however, she returned to Norway to spend a year learning to know her kinsfolk and the country.

Miss Bernhart graduated from Augustan College at Sioux Falls in 1933, spent two years as an actress with the American Art Theatre of Chicago touring the South and Southwest, and then came to the University of North Carolina to study with The Carolina Playmakers. She is now the wife of a music professor here.

On her return to her native country and her father's boyhood home in Norway in 1930, she paid a visit to the last outpost in the far North, the impoverished little fishing settlement of Komagvaer. She writes: "The picture of the small community of people living lives barren of the simplest luxuries has remained vivid. In *Home-Longing* I have tried to give a glimpse of the wooden houses painted black with whale oil, the forbidding grey rock and the grey sea, the treeless earth, and the stolid people who inhabit that place.

"Living as they do—almost without contact with the rest of the world—these people nevertheless have a virility, independence of spirit, and an undefeated belief that the sea will next year yield her life-giving harvest of fish. When I met the woman who has been characterized as Karen I was struck by her problem of finding adjustment in the harsh life of Komagvaer. Her struggle I have endeavored to express in my play."

DENMARK: *Tarantula*

The author of our Danish play was born in Copenhagen in 1916. Kai Jurgensen's father acquired consider-

able wealth during the first World War making trench
coats and was able thereby to buy a castle on the Island
of Fuen. There the author spent the first six summers of
his life. He still recalls the "huge, old rooms with stone
walls and secret passages veiled in dark, impenetrable
mystery . . . tales of ghosts and of a raped girl who left
a blood smudge on the wall of the blue chamber and
then leapt to her death in the courtyard below."

The author's early life was spent with Swedish nurses
and in private schools. And then his father lost his money.
When Jurgensen was sixteen, he came to the United
States to live with his aunt in Montana. He went to high
school and the University and there got some basic training in the theatre. In 1937 he returned to Copenhagen
and spent two years playing small parts at the Royal
Theatre. When he came back to the United States, he
worked for two years with a stamp dealer in New York
City, and then obtained a Graduate Assistantship at the
University of North Carolina. Here he wrote *Tarantula*
and several other plays, four of which were produced,
including his full-length *Down to the Sea*. He married
a girl with whom he had played in the university productions at Montana, and he is now a member of the faculty
of the Department of Dramatic Art at Carolina.

Kai Jurgensen and Robert Schenkkan (author of
Black Piet in this volume) are the editors of a new
anthology, *Fourteen Plays for the Church*.

Mr. Jurgensen tells how he got the impressions out of
which he made *Tarantula*. "The idea for the play origi-
nated in a short notice in the Copenhagen newspaper
Politiken. The notice ran somewhat like this: 'A Tarantula has been seen on the docks of Free Harbor. It un-
doubtedly arrived in a load of bananas.' Nothing more
was said about it, and probably only a very few people
even read it.

"During the winter 1938-39," writes Mr. Jurgensen, "I worked in a harbor-cafe in Copenhagen as a waiter. It was a very colorless cafe where nothing particular happened. The laborers came in for their 'half coffee' (half coffee and half Schnapps), smoked, talked; some became my friends, gave me a short glimpse of their lives—and left again. There was one among them, however, whom I remember more vividly than the rest, a man by the name of Anders, who felt, deep in his heart, a gnawing pain of inferiority. He was a 'Kul-Lemper,' a carrier of coal. When the ships came in from all over the world, laden with exotic cargoes and strange and colorful people, he carried coal aboard in a basket on his back, getting every time a glimpse of something wild and beautiful beyond the dirty docks on which he lived and worked. He was a strange man, quiet and calm and naive like a child, and dirty and profane as only the lowborn and the outcast can become—coarse and rough, and gentle. He played the piano with his clumsy, dirty fingers, playing with a depth of feeling such as only one with a real sense of the beauty of music possesses. His loves and his hates were fierce, unbounded by laws of God or man.

"Perhaps this man is my Anders. At any rate something of him has gone into the character."

South Africa: *Black Piet*

The author of the South African play was born in New York in 1917. His parents, however, are native Dutch. They came from Amsterdam in 1910, and the language of the Netherlands is still spoken in their home. Many of the friends of the family and some relatives are from South Africa, people who still enjoy talking heatedly about the Boer War. The author picked up his material for *Black Piet* from listening to them.

After graduating from high school in 1933, Robert

Schenkkan spent a summer in Holland. He worked four years in a bank; then entered the University of Virginia, where he was associated with the dramatic group under Professor Roger Boyle—acting, directing, designing and building scenery, getting several of his plays produced, winning the Raven Award, and acquiring a Phi Beta Kappa key. In 1941, he received an appointment as a Rockefeller Assistant in the Department of Dramatic Art at the University of North Carolina. His graduate work was interrupted by the war, during which he served in the Navy as a bomb disposal officer; but in 1946 Mr. Schenkkan got his Master's degree, and he is now an instructor in the Radio Department at the University. Among the parts in Playmaker productions played by the author when he was a student was the Emperor in Lily T'ang's *The Wandering Dragon.* Jean McKenzie, who was Lee Fong Fong, is now Mrs. Schenkkan.

"*Black Piet,*" the author says, "is the story of the irreconcilable warrior, the man who holds inflexibly to a narrow ideal, while the world moves on to a newer dream. It is set during the Boer War, because that struggle, with its inconclusive conclusion, produced so many Piets, men defeated but unconvinced. Piet's tragedy is that he continues to cling to the vision which inspired him when the war began, 'defender of the homeland,' and that in so doing he finds himself, at the last, arrayed no longer against the enemy but against his own people."

Mr. Schenkkan has expanded this one-act portrait of Black Piet into a full-length drama, *Not Often to the Arrogant.*

Syria: *Fleas and Figs*

Mary-Averett Seelye, theatre director at the Washington Workshop Cooperative of Washington, D. C., spent her childhood in the Mediterranean seaport, Beirut, Lebanon, where her father was a professor at the American University. It was a city of conglomerate nationalities—Lebanese, French, Armenians, British, and Americans. Aside from the usual school dramatics, there was little to substitute for present-day movies except for what the street offered in the way of an occasional peep-show man, or a Bedouin dancing girl with her drummer, or, best of all, a trained bear or monkey. Camping in the summer-time among olive trees and vineyards in the Lebanon Mountains, however, introduced the author to the colorful villagers she suggests in her play. Although the story is a bit of humorous folklore out of northern Syria, the playwright has not attempted to preserve the authenticity of the setting.

Miss Seelye explains, "The story that inspired this play is one they tell in the Near East. Whether it is true or not is one of those questions that will never be solved. The play might be set in the Lebanon Mountains where I spent a number of my early years. As with most moun-tain peoples, life here rotates around basic values with which most of the folklore deals.

"The exclamations and forms of expression in the play are as near those actually used by the people as it is pos-sible to translate them. 'Allah' is the Arabic for 'God,' and their use of it in exclamations is an accepted part of the language. The women in the mountains still use the veil on their heads to draw across their faces when a man appears, although in places this has become only a gesture. The man of the household is the accepted master, and marriages are almost always arranged affairs between families. Preparing food is an all-day enterprise, and it is considered almost impolite not to accept food when visiting in a house.

"The people of Syria are less apt to conceal their emo-tions than we are, which gives their life a colorfulness we never experience. Humor is on the alert and living is a career."

CHINA: *The Wandering Dragon*

T'ang Wen Shun (known in Chapel Hill as Lily T'ang) of Tientsin, China, received her A.B. degree in English from Yen Ching University in Peking in 1940 and the Master of Arts degree from Mount Holyoke College in Massachusetts in 1941. In the fall of that year she came to the University of North Carolina to study playwriting under Professor Koch.

Miss T'ang comes from a distinguished Buddhist family in old Canton. They worshipped at the ancestral shrine in their own Family Temple, where the history of the T'ang family is recorded for four hundred years. From early childhood she was tutored in the Chinese classics, poetry, and philosophy. She remembers crying herself to sleep many a night in her effort to memorize the sayings of the master, Confucius. As a high school girl she wrote articles for the local newspaper and for the school periodical, also, a great many *tse* (free verse) and short stories in dialogue. From the time she was a little girl, she attended the Chinese theatre regularly with her mother and learned many of the classics by heart. She was charmed by the Chinese opera and the traditional folk tales of old China.

The Wandering Dragon gets its story from a Chinese opera entitled *The Town of Mai Lung*. It follows the legend of a romantic adventure of the Emperor, Cheng Te of Ta Ming, Lord of Ten Thousand Years, who often traveled over the country in disguise. In the present play he comes to the tiny town of Mai Lung in the province of Chiangsi in South China and is enamored of the lovely Lee Fong Fong, sister of the Innkeeper. The play concludes, as does the legend, with the Emperor's setting out for his Capital with Lee Fong Fong as his adored bride, Empress of all China.

CANADA: *The Courting of Marie Jenvrin*

In the fall of 1937, a little soft-spoken Canadian girl, Gwen Pharis, came to North Carolina to study play-writing. Recipient of a Rockefeller Fellowship from the prairie province of Alberta, she wrote at the University several plays about her own people. Four of these were produced by The Carolina Playmakers: *Still Stands the House, One Man's House, Chris Axelson—Blacksmith*, and *Pasque Flower. Still Stands the House* was awarded first prize at the annual Dominion Drama Festival at Ottawa in 1939, where it was judged to be the best Canadian play submitted.

After Gwen Pharis returned to Canada, she married a young doctor and went to the far north to live in the frontier mining town of Goldfields, Saskatchewan, nearly a thousand miles above the border.

The idea for *The Courting of Marie Jenvrin* occurred to the author while she was studying her new cookbook looking for desserts that did not need whipped cream. "In this barren land, fresh milk and cream come to have a dream-like significance symbolizing all the clamorous joys of the world 'outside,' " she wrote.

The incident mentioned in the play of flying a cow in by plane is not an exaggeration. For all but two months of the year, when the Hudson's Bay freight boats come by river and lake, the only way a cow can be brought into this remote land of rock and pine is by air. "Flying cows around is expensive," the playwright says, "and much as we might yearn for the sight of that velvety-eyed animal, we 'make do' with canned milk and a cream-maker.

"Life in a country so remote from civilization presents

strong contrasts. While a trapper may charter a twin-motor plane in September to fly himself, dogs, and supplies into the barren lands to his trap line, once he is there life is a grim struggle for survival. He traverses the miles of snow and rock and muskeg moss by dog team, alone. If he is caught in a blizzard or breaks a leg while mushing from one cabin to another, or develops acute appendicitis or runs out of supplies, he dies. And until after 'break-up' in the spring no one knows that he is dead.

"If the people in the play seem a bit eccentric, it is because they have lived in the North country so long that they are 'bushed.' That is, they are unhappy anywhere except in the North. Last spring after three months 'outside' I was extremely glad to get on the plane for the Yellowknife, so perhaps—. Of course some people are 'bushed' before they come in! ..."

Mexico: *The Red Velvet Goat*

Josephina Niggli was born in Monterrey, Nuevo Leon, Mexico. Her father was a prominent manufacturer of glassware, and her mother a concert violinist and teacher of music to children. Her home throughout her girlhood was an old Mexican estate with a *casa grande* (great house), *La Quinta del Carmen*, "The Garden of Flowers," of many acres and many servants. The favorite in the family was her grandmother, affectionately known to everyone as *La Mamá*. On Sunday evenings an orchestra conducted by the gardener's son-in-law would come to the house and say, "We have come to serenade *La Mamá*!" Then everyone would have to stop what he was doing and listen to the music.

Miss Niggli received her early literary training at Incarnate Word College, at San Antonio, Texas, where she was much encouraged in her writing by Dr. R. E. Roehl, Head of the English Department. She had already had some of her verse published when she came to the University of North Carolina to do graduate work in 1935. Here Miss Niggli wrote one-act plays about her native Mexico, seven of which The Carolina Playmakers produced: *Tooth or Shave, Soldadera, Azteca, Sunday Costs Five Pesos, The Cry of Dolores, This Is Villa,* and *The Red Velvet Goat,* which is included in this volume. The Playmakers produced also two of Miss Niggli's full-length plays: *Singing Valley* and *The Fair-God.* After her graduation she served at the University for a year as Instructor in Radio. Josephina Niggli is now living with her mother in Chapel Hill, where she is busily pursuing her writing. Besides short stories, she has published five books: *Mexican Folk Plays, Pointers on Playwriting, Pointers on Radio Writing,* and two novels, *Mexican Village* and *Step Down, Elder Brother.* Miss Niggli's plays have appeared in twelve American and English anthologies.

The Red Velvet Goat is a *saenete,* a Spanish type of farce unknown to the English-speaking stage but very popular in Mexico. The author explains: "The true *saenete* is a picture of what we call the 'lower classes' lifted from reality to the stage. It is written in poetic dialogue, it is a comedy, and it has a romantic flavor.

"It is a home-made play such as one can see in any village from Quintana Roo to the Rio Grande. When a Mexican goes to a play he goes, not as a spectator, but with the firm intention of being as much a part of the drama as the actors on the stage. It is the prompter, however, who bears the full burden of the performance; and so, to him, health and wealth!

"All of the characters, with the exception of Mariana, are drawn from life. Esteban, whose real name I have forgotten, I often used to see at dances playing a saxophone which he had bought from a Sears, Roebuck catalogue, because, as he said, it looked so much like a worm. He called it a 'sasafona,' and when he blew into the mouthpiece it rested with God as to what note would come out at the other end.

"Lorenzo, Ester, Don Pepe, Doña Berta, are all people whom I have known and loved since infancy. I can still see in memory the various Esters sitting primly at dances while their fans flashed back and forth in signals at the various Lorenzos grouped about the doors, while the Doña Bertas sat in magnificent grandeur ready to pounce on the first couple which did not behave in a manner befitting young ladies and gentlemen."

The Red Velvet Goat is one of Miss Niggli's most popular plays. It has been widely produced both in the United States and in England.

THE UNITED STATES (JEWISH): *Wherefore Is This Night*

Violet Fidel was born in Brooklyn, New York City, in 1927, of college-educated Russo-American parents. She grew up in the city "with occasional visits to 'country' places like New Jersey" and attended Hunter and Barnard Colleges and Columbia University. In the fall of 1945 she came to Chapel Hill to finish her college course, and it was here that she began writing plays, three of which, *Niobe in Darkness*, *Wherefore Is This Night*, and *Hunter from the Hill*, were presented by the Playmakers. In 1945 she received the Frederick H. Koch Playwriting Scholarship.

Wherefore Is This Night deals with the problem of foreign born and foreign parented Jews who are culturally "neither fish nor fowl." Miss Fidel says: "What it does to a person to have to lie all his life, like Jack, or to cling tenaciously to something that doesn't exist any-more—like Mr. Lewissohn—there's tragedy there. And beneath it all sound the minor overtones of a song that

the ancient Hebrews sang long ago, still beautiful. But
who can forget that outside the window is Newark, New
Jersey, U.S.A., 20th Century?

"There are no villains in my play, because I do not
think there are any real villains in the world. It's just a
question of incomplete understanding—the Socratic idea
that no man can do evil voluntarily. And maybe through
plays we can gain a better understanding. That is to me
the primary mission of the theatre."

THE UNITED STATES (NEGRO): *Washed in de Blood*

The author of *Washed in de Blood* is one of the two
playwrights in this book who do not belong to the national or racial group about which they write. (The
other is Miss Seelye.) Rietta Bailey is a white girl, but
she knows the Negroes intimately. She comes from the
little town of Cochran in middle Georgia. She graduated
from Wesleyan College, in Macon, in 1934, and became
a case worker for the Federal Emergency Relief Administration in Harris County. There and in the Pine
Mountain Valley Rural Community she worked among
the farm laborers, both black and white. For six weeks
she did relief work in the textile strike at LaGrange;
then in 1936 she went on to the Recreational Division of
the Works Progress Administration in West Georgia,
traveling over several counties organizing recreation pro-
grams. The next year she came to the University of
North Carolina to do graduate work. She wrote plays,
two of which were produced by The Carolina Playmakers; and she studied dancing. For four summer sea-
sons she was a principal dancer in Paul Green's historical
play, *The Lost Colony*, on Roanoke Island. She married
Fred Howard, who staged the dances and acted the role
of Uppowoc, the Indian Medicine Man.

Of the people in her play the young author says, "I

think I have known about Negro sinning and Negro
religion as long as I have known about anything. My
mammy told me tales about 'de Lawd' and 'de heabenly
glory.' Her faith was as much a part of her everyday life
as her work.

"Aunt Angeline was the oldest person I have ever seen.
She mumbled to herself all day. She was wise and kind.
She had a strange power which seemed to put her in
touch with things beyond this world. Sappory cooked
for us. She went to Atlanta one week-end and sinned a
little, and came home worried about it. She was sure she
could make it all right with 'de Lawd' if she prayed and
repented. She did. Once she got 'stobbed' on a Saturday
night coming home from a dance, but she didn't com-
plain. Liza still lives in a very clean cabin down the lane
from us. She is the best moaner I have ever heard."

The songs in her play the author heard at Mount Zion
Church in her home town. She says, "I cannot sing them
as they came to me, nor can any white person. There is
a beauty, a haunting, unfinished melody, which varies
every time the songs are sung. There is no music which
comes as freely, as naturally as this."

Commenting on Miss Bailey's play, Professor Koch re-
marked: "Here is something new in our Southern folk
drama. Former Playmakers have made effective use of the
emotional excitement of the Negro church services.
Frank Durham has presented the frenzied worship of the
brass ankles of South Carolina. These plays remind us of
the medieval Mystery Plays of religious brotherhoods
which were designed to vivify the Bible stories for the
unlettered audiences of the Dark Ages. Miss Bailey's
drama suggests also the Miracle and Morality Plays of
the same period, more specifically the latter. She uses, not
a story of Bible characters or saints' miracles, but an ab-
stract moral idea—the salvation of man by faith."

CONTENTS

xxiii

NORWAY

HOME-LONGING

BY *Gerd Bernhart*

THE CHARACTERS

As originally produced by The Carolina Playmakers on their Thirty-fourth Bill of Experimental Productions of New Plays in the Playmakers Theatre, Chapel Hill, North Carolina, October 31, 1935.

KAREN NIELSEN .... THE AUTHOR
IDA OLSEN, *a neighbor* .... JANIE BRITT
PASTOR JACOBSEN .... KENNETH BARTLETT
TANTE ANNA KJERLOFF, *Karen's aunt*
                                SAMMIE RUTH BELL
BORGHILD STRAND, *a neighbor* .... BEVERLY HAMER
AAGOT OLSEN, *Ida's daughter* .... CAROLINE HOUSE
ERLING NIELSEN, *husband of Karen* ... CHARLES LLOYD
KARL PEDERSON, *a fisherman* ...... WILLIAM FLETCHER

THE SCENE: A small northern settlement in Norway. The living-room of the Nielsens' home in Komagvaer.

THE TIME: One o'clock. An afternoon in the latter part of July, 1930.

THE SCENE

The scene is laid on the fringe of the world, in KAREN *and* ERLING NIELSEN'S *best room in their home at Komagvaer, Norway. Well-worn, spotless curtains frame the small window at the rear which looks out upon a gray sea. To the left of the window is a tall chest of drawers, on the top of which is a copper coffeepot and a small Norwegian flag on a tiny pole. The inevitable Norwegian coffee table with a chair beside it is placed down left. On the right is evidence of expected guests in the formal placement of three chairs and a footstool. The door on left stage is the one leading to that room in the building which serves as stable for the goat as well as general storeroom. The other door, up right, leads to the edge of the rock cliff on which the house is built. Outside can be heard the continuous beat of the waves of the never-still Arctic sea.*

The rising curtain shows us KAREN NIELSEN, *attractively attired in soft-toned linen and a multicolored coffee apron.* KAREN *looks about thirty years old. Notwithstanding the outmoded fashion of her "ear-puff" hairdress, which she has remembered to be the height of fashion in a time gone by, she makes a becoming picture.* KAREN *gives the impression of softness, in striking contrast to the sturdiness of the native-born people of Komagvaer. She is sweeping by the door, when she sees someone on the strand below and calls:*

3

KAREN. Hallo—Karl Pederson.

VOICE OF PEDERSON (*offstage*). Hallo, you. A fine day to you.

KAREN. That it is, Karl Pederson.

KARL. And handsome you look this morning, girl.

KAREN. Today, Karl Pederson—today is Tante Anna coming from Tönsberg.

KARL. Oh, ja—ja, I know.

KAREN. Come in for coffee this afternoon, Karl Pederson. (*She continues her sweeping a moment, then looks up and calls.*) Ida, Ida Olsen, good morning to you.

VOICE OF IDA OLSEN (*offstage*). Good morning. Thank you for the last time.

KAREN. Thank you. Leave your sweeping and come over, Ida.

VOICE OF IDA OLSEN. Ja—well.
(KAREN *turns back into the room, humming gaily. She goes to the chest of drawers and brings out cups and saucers.*)
(IDA OLSEN *appears in the doorway. She is an ungraceful forty-five, hiding a good heart under a "I-have-a-grudge-against-everything" exterior. She is dressed in shapeless gray. Her hair is brought to an uncompromising knot on the top of her head. She has a habit of emphasizing her remarks by viciously jabbing the combs she wears.*)

IDA. Ja—well. I suppose you are happy today. Now we shall see the Tante Anna you have told us so much about.

KAREN. Think of it, Ida—it is seven years ago that Erling and I were married—seven years, and never have we left Komagvaer. And never till today has anyone from the South come here. (*She holds up a piece of linen.*) Shall I use this Hardanger? [1] This morning early I made Krumkaker [2]—see. (*Then, glimpsing* AAGOT, *age eleven, dressed in a drab dress with white apron, who has been standing timidly in the doorway.*) Oh, come in, Aagot. Would you like a Krumkake?
(AAGOT *smiles, curtsies, and takes one of the cakes. She sits on the stool by* IDA's *feet.*)

IDA (*crossing over to the chair on the right she seats herself*). Such extravagance! And with everything so dear. No fish last year and no fish this year—oh jason. [3]

AAGOT (*eating her cake with delight*). Oh Karen, you look beautiful!

KAREN (*turning around to show off her dress*). You like it, child? Erling bought it for me when we were first married, before we came to Komagvaer. Oh, I remember so well—it was Madam Hammer's store. She showed dress after dress, such beautiful materials—silk—

AAGOT. Really silk?

1. A table cover of open fancywork, like heavy lace, made in the valley of Hardanger.
2. Cakes shaped like ice cream cones.
3. A Norwegian interjection, similar to the English *well*.

KAREN. Ja, really silk. We couldn't afford silk, of course, but this we got of nice linen.

IDA (*she walks over to* KAREN). Let's feel it. (*She takes the cloth of the dress in her fingers.*) Ja. (*Grudgingly.*) It is quite good.

KAREN (*laughing*). After today, Ida, you may have it. I'm sure I should only be buried in it.

IDA (*reprimandingly*). Such talk! And before Aagot. Now, tell me, is coffee made for your Tante?

KAREN. Ja—made, and with a whole egg in it.

IDA. Egg in it? Now, that is too much. You tempt the trolls with such extravagance, that you do. Poor Erling.

KAREN (*sobering*). Ja, perhaps Poor Erling. But in the seven years I've lived in Komagvaer never have we had egg in the coffee until today, and only once before have we had Krumkaker.

IDA. And right that is, with no fish last year and no fish this year, and only the Lord God knows when they will come.

KAREN (*remembering the past, fondly*). Erling and I, we used to have such gay things at home in Tönsberg.

IDA. You live in Komagvaer, not Tönsberg.

KAREN (*continuing as though she had not heard* IDA). At home in Tönsberg, Erling and I went to the cafe, and we sang and danced.

IDA. Jason—singing and dancing! Life is heavy here in Komagvaer.

KAREN (*with a sigh*). Ja—heavy. I can remember so well the first time we went to the theatre together, Grand Theatre. There was music, oh, such music. Never have I heard such music. (*Shyly.*) You know I used to play when I was a girl.

AAGOT. What did you play?

KAREN. Oh, a little on the piano.

AAGOT (*excitedly*). Could you teach me to play?

KAREN. Ja, little one. (*Turning back to the coffee table.*) But here there is no piano.

AAGOT. But—(IDA *claps her hand over* AAGOT's *mouth and leads her to the door, speaking as she goes.*)

IDA. Borghild is having us all for the evening meal, you know. Come, Aagot.

KAREN (*following* IDA *and* AAGOT *to the door*). Ja, adieu, Ida. Everyone must come for coffee.
(*From offstage can be heard greetings exchanged between* IDA *and* ERLING NIELSEN, *who appears in the door carrying a fishnet and string.* ERLING *is lean and salty looking. His hair, eyes, and skin, are all of a tannish-red hue, acquired from constant exposure to the northern sea. As he comes in he looks questioningly at* KAREN.)

ERLING. Ja, well, are we almost ready for Anna?

KAREN. Ja, it is a shame she couldn't arrive here this morning.

ERLING (*walking over to the downstage chair on right. He sits and begins to mend the net*). No, only the freight got off this morning. All passengers must wait until after noonday. (KAREN *is humming gaily as she prepares the coffee table.*) Happy, girl?

KAREN. Oh, Erling, as I've never been. Think, Tante Anna comes all the way from Tönsberg to see us and she will tell us—

ERLING (*with a touch of bitterness*). Ja, she will tell us that in Tönsberg they have all the fish they can use and some to throw in the fjord.

KAREN. Oh, you and the fish!

ERLING. It's fish we live by, girl. Don't forget that.

KAREN. No, I don't forget it. I couldn't. All we do is talk of fish that don't come—never of anything but fish.

ERLING. It hasn't been easy for you, I know.

KAREN (*repentantly*). It's that it has been different.

ERLING. Ja, different it is. I know, girl. I've seen you stand in the window, looking south. I have listened to you cry in the night—I know.

KAREN (*she goes over to* ERLING *and sits on the stool by his feet*). It's the waves—for long I thought surely I should go mad with the waves always knocking like trolls against the rock.

ERLING. Ja, like trolls.

KAREN. And the winters, Erling, the dark winters when we live here day and night with oil lamps that blow out when the wind comes through the door.

ERLING. But we have the midnight sun. From all the world, folk come to see the midnight sun.

KAREN. But not to Komagvaer. No one ever comes to Komagvaer. And the midnight sun is so short flowers and trees can't grow. (*Turning to him suddenly.*) Don't you miss them, Erling?

ERLING (*simply*). No, girl.

KAREN (*dropping her voice sadly*). No, you weren't born in the South. There we have trees and flowers. (*Her face brightening.*) You remember the feast days in Tönsberg, Erling? St. Hans Eve, when all the children carried flags, and we built such big fires and sang "Naar Fjordene Blaaner Som Markens Fiol"? Oh, we were gay—and the music! It's the music I've missed most, Erling.

ERLING (*with quiet satisfaction*). The music, that's good.

KAREN. Good, you say? (*Passionately.*) And I say it's not good to have nothing but fish and waves, waves and fish.

ERLING. Now, girl, I didn't mean that.

KAREN. Once we were gay, Erling. (*After a moment.*) Don't you ever think about that time you came South with Captain Haakonson's fishing boat? Don't you remember when we went to Haakonson's house and played? (*Softly*.) You asked me to marry you that night, Erling.

ERLING. Ja, I remember. (*He puts his hand fondly, a little shyly, on her shoulder*.) Perhaps sorry you have been.

KAREN. Oh, no, no, Erling. You are a good husband. (ERLING *accepts the compliment with some embarrassment*.) I have only longed sometime for what I knew —pretty sounds—a little color. Not always waves and fish. (*Then quickly*.) But you, Erling, you are good.

ERLING. Ja, well. Did you put Lillebel to pasture?

KAREN (*jumping up aghast*). Oh, God help us! Today has been so busy that never did I think of Lillebel. I'll take her now. (*She starts for the door on left stage leading to the stable*.)

ERLING (*rising and going past her*). No, I'll get her. (*In a moment he returns, with a goat which he leads over to the outside door, up right*.) Come, Lillebel, come, Lillebel.

KAREN (*who has followed her husband*). Erling, the boat should soon be in. You will be there to meet it?

ERLING. Ja. (*As he starts to go out*.) Oh, here is Pastor Jacobsen.
(KAREN *hurriedly removes her apron, and throws it over a chair, and goes to the door to shake hands with* PASTOR JACOBSEN. ERLING *tethers Lillebel outside and re-enters to greet the* PASTOR. *The* PASTOR *is dressed*

in dusty black—a gray man with a gray moustache, and a stiff manner.)

JACOBSEN. Good day, Fru Nielsen. Thank you for the last time.

KAREN. Good day. Thank *you* for the last time. (*Motioning him politely toward a chair.*) Sit down, Pastor Jacobsen.

ERLING. Good day, Pastor Jacobsen. Thank you for the last time.

JACOBSEN. Thank you. (*Stepping into the room.*) Well, well, this is a big day for you, isn't it?

KAREN. Ja, that it is. Sit down—sit here.
(*She indicates a chair on left stage. The* PASTOR *sits stiffly, and* KAREN *seats herself beside him.* ERLING *stays by the door.*)

JACOBSEN. Ja, a big day for you this must be.

ERLING. Karen here has been so excited she hasn't slept for nights. Excuse me, Pastor Jacobsen, while I put Lillebel to pasture.

JACOBSEN. Ja, ja. (ERLING *leaves.* JACOBSEN, *turning to* KAREN.) We missed you at church service last Sunday, Fru Nielsen. You must not let your excitement make you forget the house of God.

KAREN. Oh, Pastor, it was not that. But the storm tore Erling's net so badly that I had to mend it till late in the night.

JACOBSEN. That was a storm. But God sent it to us and His gifts are good.

KAREN. Ja, Pastor—and sometimes I think that even storms are better than steady waves always pounding on the rock. (*She turns her face toward the sea.*)

JACOBSEN (*slightly disconcerted at finding his wisdom taken in this unexpected way*). Hmmm—today is important for you, is it not, Fru Nielsen?

KAREN. Oh, ja. Today have we been so busy. (*Laughing.*) I even forgot to put Lillebel to pasture.

JACOBSEN. One must not forget one's duty, Fru Nielsen. (*Smiling a little.*) But it is good to see you happy. You have never found your lot among us easy.

KAREN. It is not easy to be happy in one place when you long to be in another. Haven't you ever been sad to remember your student days in the southland?

JACOBSEN. Perhaps, but God's work must be done—and then it is so long ago I have forgotten.

KAREN (*rising in agitation*). Many times have I wished to forget, but always when I look out I see black houses and gray rock and—(*By this time she has reached the door.*) Oh, Pastor, the boat—it's in! (*The* PASTOR *also goes to the door.* KAREN *speaks excitedly.*) Look, there's Erling—and that must be Tante Anna. Oh, I hope they hurry! (*Cupping her mouth with her hands.*) Hallo—

VOICES FROM BELOW. Hallo—
     (*Little* AAGOT *comes running in.*)

AAGOT. They are come, Karen. They are bringing the surprise. It is—(AAGOT *sees the* PASTOR *and automatically curtsies.*)

KAREN. Run, Aagot, get me another chair. There is one by the churn.

AAGOT. Ja, Karen. (AAGOT *runs off left.*)

JACOBSEN. Can I help you, Fru Nielsen?

KAREN. Oh no, thank you, Pastor. Just excuse me a moment. (KAREN *meets* AAGOT *in the doorway as she goes off left.*)

AAGOT (*carrying the footstool which she places in center stage. She runs excitedly to* PASTOR JACOBSEN). They are come, and do you know what they are bringing?

JACOBSEN. No, child, what?

AAGOT. Oh, it's a great surprise. It's going to be for me too. It's a—sh!
(AAGOT *is interrupted by* KAREN *who returns carrying a coffeepot which she places on the coffee table.*)

KAREN. Aagot, please put the footstool over there. (*She points to a spot on stage right. Voices are heard offstage.*) Oh, here they are, here they are! (KAREN *hurries to the door as* TANTE ANNA, BORGHILD, *and* IDA *come to view.* TANTE ANNA *is stylishly attired, a woman of fifty, soft, kind, and discontented.* BORGHILD, *about forty, is like jelly, nice but not substantial. Her overflowing body seems to symbolize the fertility of which she is so proud.* KAREN *and* TANTE ANNA *fall into each other's arms.*)

KAREN. Tante Anna. It is so strange! (*Half-laughing, half-crying.*)

ANNA (*drawing* KAREN *to the center of the room*). Let me look at you, Karen. Ja, it is you, Astrid's daughter.

KAREN. Welcome, welcome, Tante Anna. You have met these friends, Borghild Strand and Ida Olsen?

ANNA. That I have.

IDA. Of course we met.
(IDA *and* BORGHILD *go to the chairs on stage right.*)

KAREN. Fru Kjerloff, Pastor Jacobsen. (TANTE ANNA *and the* PASTOR *shake hands.*)

IDA. Does she look different, Fru Kjerloff?

ANNA. A little thinner, perhaps. (*She gazes at her niece affectionately.*) Are you happy, little Karen?

KAREN. That you are here makes me very happy. Sit down everyone. (TANTE ANNA *and the* PASTOR *sit in chairs on left stage.*) We shall have coffee, and then you must tell all about Tönsberg. (AAGOT *has been clinging shyly behind her mother.*) Tante Anna, this is little Aagot, Fru Olsen's daughter. Sit down, child, on the little chair. (*Pointing to the footstool.*)
(*During the ensuing scene* KAREN *is busy serving coffee to her guests.*)

BORGHILD. Fru Kjerloff, do you have many children?

ANNA. I had two, but they died at birth.

BORGHILD. Tsk—so sad. Perhaps you did not place a fish over the doorway.

ANNA. Fish over the doorway?

BORGHILD (*speaking with slow relish*). Ja, a fish over the doorway always makes boys grow big. Now, when I was carrying George, I was having a bad time. The fish did not come this way that year, but I took a small salmon, hung it over the doorway, and George came just like that. Oh, it is good.

IDA. Foolishness! (BORGHILD *retires in a huff*.) I suppose Komagvaer seems very poor after Tönsberg, Frue.

ANNA. Oh, no. It is so good to get away from Tönsberg.

KAREN (*astonished*). Good to get away from Tönsberg, Tante?

ANNA. Ja, you can't think how tiresome it is getting to be. Bah—gas stations, cinema houses. Do you know, Karen, they have torn down the summer garden and have built a red and white service station there.

KAREN (*incredulously*). Not the beautiful garden where we danced on the 17th of May?

ANNA. That very one.

KAREN. Oh, but that was so beautiful.

BORGHILD. Isn't that the place you tell Aagot of where children have a pool to float ships in?

AAGOT (*with tears in her voice*). Not that one, Karen, is it?

KAREN. I'm afraid it is, little Aagot. (*Hopefully.*) But there is still the children's market on Stenmalsveien, the fine place where children play while their mothers and fathers sell their eggs and butter.

ANNA. That, too, is no longer. The town merchants have now done away with the whole market place.

KAREN (*not believing what she hears*). No market place? But there was always a market place.

ANNA. No more is there one. Now you buy in shops only. (*Drinking her coffee.*) Such good coffee this is, Karen.

KAREN. Thank you, Tante Anna. (*Her voice catching.*) You say no market place. Then where is old Jonas? I have wondered so much about old Jonas.

ANNA. Old Jonas who sold tin ware? Ja, we never see him now, for he is night watchman for an automobile company, and ailing.

KAREN. Old Jonas who told us such tall tales? (*Almost in tears.*) Oh, it is not good.

JACOBSEN. The Pastor in Tönsberg, Fru Kjerloff, does he use the thirty-seventh or the sixty-fourth service?

ANNA. Oh, the good days are gone when you went to church and heard the word of God. Now they talk of politics, and the Storting,[1] and of science. I seldom go to church any more.

1. The Norwegian parliament.

JACOBSEN. Think then! It does not seem possible, Frue. You picture a sorry scene, a sorry scene.

IDA. I should like to hear about the kvindeforening,[2] where the women sew and bake for the poor.

BORGHILD. Karen has told us of the fine time she had there. You told us about going to kvindeforening with your mother, you remember, Karen?

KAREN (*leaning forward anxiously*). Ja.

ANNA. Well, that too has changed. Now they have a social worker. (*Sighing.*) Ah, the church in Tönsberg is not what it was.

KAREN (*almost afraid to ask*). But the Grand Theatre, Tante Anna, there surely must be music and gay folk as I knew them, ja?

ANNA (*quietly*). The Grand Theatre has been made into a cinema house.
(KAREN *has been listening to the recital of the changes in her beloved girlhood home in the way a child might listen to statements which are destroying her long-held faith in the Santa Claus legend.*)

KAREN (*after a moment*). Then where is the music, Tante Anna?

AAGOT. Can't I tell her, Mama?

IDA. Hush, child.

2. The ladies' aid society of the Lutheran church.

KAREN. Tell me what, little Aagot?
(BORGHILD *and* IDA *start talking together to cover the break*.)

IDA. It seems to me that—

BORGHILD. The midwife is coming to Freda Rommer to-day. Do you know, Fru Kjerloff, that the poor woman has dreamt of whales for a week on end. A sad thing, for if a woman dreams of whales, her child will drown before it is a year old.

ANNA (*amused*). So? That is sad. (*Turning to* KAREN.) Karen, child, when shall you visit us in Tönsberg?

KAREN. When? I don't know, Tante Anna. It is so far and the fish don't come. But how I should love it! I'd go to listen to string quartettes every Wednesday—it is on Wednesday that they still play, isn't it—Hans and Karl and the others?

ANNA. No, child. You see Hans and Karl left Tönsberg to go to America, and so we have no string quartettes, now.

KAREN (*with protest in her voice*). No, Tante Anna! Is everything changed that I knew? It is not *so* long that I've been away from Tönsberg.

ANNA (*disconsolately*). Sometimes it seems to me that everything is changed. But then, I'm getting old.

BORGHILD. Oh no, Frue. Why, last May, the woman Tapio who must be almost sixty summers had a fine baby boy. Of course she's a Lap and she knew about hanging the salmon over the doorway.

IDA. And better she'd never had it, that you know, Borg-hild.

(*During* BORGHILD's *speech* KARL PEDERSON *and* ERLING *have appeared in the doorway.* KAREN *has gone to greet them.* KARL PEDERSON *might have stepped out of an old Flemish picture, even to the gray sideburns growing low on his jowls. He has on boots, a shapeless canvas hat, and a heavy dark flannel shirt.* KARL PEDERSON *is of the best the sea can produce. Hearty, broad, delighting in fooling the credulous, a man of sixty-five who has no age.*)

KARL (*stepping into the room and turning to* TANTE ANNA). Good-day again, Frue. (*Makes a deep bow. To* IDA.) What shall we do with it? (IDA *motions silence.*) Oh—(*With an understanding look toward* KAREN.) Ja, and what did I hear Borghild say she knew as we came in? Something about a childbirth, I'll wager. (BORGHILD *sniffs her annoyance.*) Now, Fru Kjerloff, have you been telling our Karen all about her beloved Tönsberg?

ANNA. About Tönsberg we have talked.

KARL. Once when I was young I was there, and a time we had.

AAGOT. What did you do there, Karl Pederson?

KARL. Oh, I was a miraculous fellow then, let me tell you.

AAGOT. But what did you do, Karl Pederson?

KARL. All day we sailed the fjord, and I was as good as any three men, you can believe, and all night we danced and sang in the grand cafes. (*Savoring the memory*.) Ja, there we had beer and aquavit, and there were fine girls, that you can know.

JACOBSEN (*muttering*). Girls and aquavit!

KARL (*with an eye on the* PASTOR). All this we did, but Sunday saw us in Tönsberg's church, Aagot. Ja, there we were, singing with the best.

KAREN. A cup of coffee, Karl?

KARL. Thank you, Karen.

ANNA. How long will the midnight sun last, Erling?

ERLING. It will be some weeks now, and then we must start burning oil, for a while only at night and then all day.

ANNA. Think of it! And it will be dark till summer?

ERLING. Oh no, in the spring we get light in the day again. (KAREN *has been collecting the coffee cups from her guests*.)

KAREN. Ja, but the winters are so long. Tante Anna, how is the family of Captain Haakonson?

ANNA. Didn't I write you? So sad, the Captain lost his ships and sails for a whaler. Stenner and Gunnar went to America.

KAREN (*stopping unhappily*). Oh no, Tante Anna. Is nothing left in Tönsberg as I knew it?
(*She turns to the coffee table to hide her distress*.)

JACOBSEN. God creates, man destroys.

ANNA. Truly. (*Glancing at* KAREN.) Erling, shan't we have the surprise I brought for Karen?

ERLING. It is here, Tante Anna.
(ERLING *and* KARL PEDERSON *go outside and return shortly with a small harmonium, a reed organ.* AAGOT, *at the mention of the surprise, has run to* KAREN.)

AAGOT. Ja, Karen, it is lovely.

KAREN. Now, but what? What is it? An organ! (*With joyful surprise.*) Oh, no, it can't be!

IDA. And why can't it be?

AAGOT (*jumping excitedly*). You said you would teach me to play, Karen.

KAREN. Tante Anna, for me?

ANNA. For you, Karen. Erling told me you would like it.

KAREN. Oh, Erling! (*Hugging* TANTE ANNA.) Oh, thank you a thousand times.

IDA. I don't suppose you can play "Aa Kjore Vatten"?

BORGHILD. Ja, can you that one? I used to sing that to Johann when his teeth were coming through. It was the only thing that helped him.

JACOBSEN. Fru Nielsen, do you play "Den Store Hvite Flok"?

KARL. Let us have "Per Spelmann."

(KAREN *at the organ plays "Aa Kjore Vatten." Every-*
one joins in the song, IDA in a high falsetto, BORGHILD
with a vague but sweet tone. KARL PEDERSON uses
much foot stamping and arm waving. ERLING sings
true, as does TANTE ANNA. The PASTOR has a tendency
to hang on to his notes.)

Aa kjore Vatten aa kjore Ve
Aa kjore Tommer over Heia
Aa kjore hvem som kjore vil,
Jeg kjore Henta mi eja.

De rode Rose aa de Oine blaa,
De vakkre Jenter holder je uttaa,
Helst naar je faar den je vil ha,
Saa er det morosamt aa leva.

BORGHILD (*sentimentally*). Oh, it reminds me of Johann's teeth.

KARL. Now that was good.

KAREN (*she is almost overcome with happiness in her gift*). I am so happy, I can't say it.

JACOBSEN. Think then, we can have music for our church service.

AAGOT. And you will teach me to play, Karen, you said.

IDA. Hush, child. We will all forget our work with this new instrument.

KARL. But you like it, eh, Ida?

IDA. Of course I like it.

BORGHILD. It is fine. It grows late. Fru Kjerloff, you are to come to my house for the evening meal, all of you are to come.

ANNA. Thank you, Frue.

JACOBSEN (*he draws out a heavy gold watch*). It is growing late.

KARL. Let us have "Per Spelmann" before we go. Come, Karen.

(KAREN *agrees and all sing "Per Spelmann."*)

Per Spelmann, han hadde ei einaste Ku,
Per Spelmann, han hadde ei einaste Ku.
Han bytta bort Kua, fekk Fela igjen,
Han bytta bort Kua, fekk Fela igjen!
Du gamle, go'e Fiolin,
Du Fiolin, du Fela mi!

IDA. Now we must go.

AAGOT. You will teach me, won't you?

KAREN (*putting her arms around the child*). I will like to teach you, little Aagot.

BORGHILD. Come, Aagot. Come, Karen.

KAREN (*turning to* ANNA). Tante Anna, will you please go with Borghild and Ida? I will be with you in a minute.

ANNA. Of course, Karen.

KAREN (*takes* ANNA's *hand*). Thank you! Thank you! (ANNA *and* KAREN *embrace*.) Thank you!

IDA. Ja, come, Fru Kjerloff, or our fish will be spoiled. Can you get good fish in Tönsberg, Frue? (*All the guests are leaving in general commotion*.)

KARL (*shakes* KAREN's *hand*). Thank you for coffee, Karen.

JACOBSEN (*also shakes* KAREN's *hand*). Thank you, Fru Nielsen. It is fine to have the organ. We must thank God for our blessings.

ERLING (*has gone outside the door and can be heard calling after the departing guests*). You must watch the stones; the last storm washed some away. (KAREN *has walked back to the organ. She stands a moment caressing it, then sits, starts to play "Paa Solen Jeg Ser," and overcome with emotion, she breaks and cries in her arms*. ERLING *returns to the room*.)

ERLING. Why, girl, now I thought you would be happy.

KAREN. I am so happy, Erling, and a little sad.

ERLING. But I thought this would make you happy.

KAREN. And you were right. Oh, Erling, that you thought of this for me. (*Touching the organ*.) It is beautiful!

ERLING. But then, girl, why are you sad?

KAREN. Did you hear what Tante Anna told? The summer garden is a gas station; the Grand Theatre a cinema; no string quartette; my friends are gone. Erling, you said you have listened to me cry in the night, and watched me look southward. For seven years, Erling. And now I know it isn't there—my Tönsberg isn't there.

ERLING. But we can have the music of the Grand Theatre right here.

KAREN (*she rises and clasps* ERLING'S *hand*). Ja, Erling. Now we can have it here. Music of the Grand Theatre. The dark winter will be lighter—and I can drown the waves with singing.

ERLING. That you can.

KAREN (*returning to her groping mood*). Think, Erling, the things I loved are not there. All changed. Why have I not known?

ERLING (*fondly*). You have been dreaming, girl, and perhaps the dreams became too real. Here nothing changes.

KAREN. No. This doesn't change. You don't change, Erling. And now we have music.

ERLING. Ja, play for me, Karen.

KAREN. We must go to Borghild's.

ERLING. Just once, Karen.

KAREN. Ja.

(*She plays a few measures of "Paa Solen Jeg Ser," and turns to smile up at* ERLING.)

CURTAIN

DENMARK
TARANTULA
BY *Kai Jurgensen*

THE CHARACTERS

*As originally produced by The Carolina Playmakers
on their Seventy-eighth Bill of Experimental Productions
of New Plays in The Playmakers Theatre, Chapel Hill,
North Carolina, November 13, 1941.*

PETREA, *a waitress* .... Lucile Culbert
ANDERS, *a young stevedore* .... Lynn Gault
HANS, *an older stevedore* .... Walter Spearman
VILHELM, *a sailor* .... Marne Snyder
THE PROFESSOR .... Frank Groseclose
* A SAILOR .... Russell Rogers
* A GIRL .... Anice Garmany

THE SCENE: A restaurant, Free Harbor, Copenhagen.

THE TIME: The present. Early afternoon in spring.

* These two characters are omitted from the printed version
of the play.

THE SCENE

The scene is a harbor-cafe in the part of Copenhagen which is called Free Harbor. It is a little, dirty room with low ceiling and heavy shutters and doors. Upstage left is a Dutch door, open at the top, and a few worn steps that lead down from street-level to the floor of the cafe. An iron railing is on the downstage side of the steps. There is an old oaken counter upstage center, extending to the stage right wall. Back of the counter, in the right wall, there is a swinging door with a dirty glass window. This door leads to the kitchen. Downstage are groups of tables with blue-and-white checkered tablecloths. Old wooden chairs are grouped around the tables.

High on the left wall is a small cellar window hung with dirty white curtains.

On the walls are beer and liquor advertisements; also a few old pictures of ships. On the floor is sand.

All through the play, from offstage come the sounds of the harbor: foghorns, bell buoys, ship bells and whistles, the soft lapping of the water, the screech of truck brakes, the ominous, murmuring hum of the huge cranes swinging along their tracks, the rattle of coal through chutes.

It is early afternoon. Pale beams of sunlight fall through the window, pierce the dust, and hit the counter and the tables; but even with that light the room is dark and gloomy.

A beam of sunlight falls through the door and hits PETREA, *the waitress, who is by the counter, polishing*

31

glasses. She takes them out of the dirty water, wipes them a bit on her apron, then holds them up to the light, trying to see through them. Then she puts them on a shelf above the counter.

PETREA *is a slovenly female; young, skinny, and dirty. Her hair is stringy and eternally falling into her eyes, so that she has to brush it away with greasy hands. Her dress is dirty-pink. She wears no stockings and her shoes are downtrodden. Her face is sharp and her voice is shrill, by virtue of which she carries a certain authority in the cafe, mostly based upon the sailors' inherent respect for the phenomenon of womanhood.*

ANDERS, *a young stevedore, appears at the Dutch door to the street. He stops outside and leans silently against the closed lower half, his elbows hooked over the edge. He looks down at* PETREA *for a short spell. Then he opens the door and enters.*

He wears a greasy cap; his hair is clipped short to keep it from flying in his eyes on a windy day. He has on a blue denim workman's blouse, corduroy trousers, and heavy brogues. He is clean-washed and shaven. His face is dark from the sun and wind, full of conflicting shadows and lines. His eyes are a little shifty. His hands fumble around the lower edge of his blouse. When he speaks, it is slowly, hesitantly. He is not used to talking much, particularly not to women.

ANDERS. You look pretty—in the sun.

PETREA (*without turning*). Nah—

ANDERS. Yah—you're good to look at.

PETREA (*coyly*). Who says so?

ANDERS. I do. (*Makes a sudden movement.* PETREA *turns.*) Can I come down?

PETREA. Certainly you can come down. This is a public restaurant. Anybody can come down. What're you standing up there for anyway?

ANDERS. Nothing.

PETREA. Well, then—come down.

ANDERS. All right. If you ask me.

PETREA. Come on down.

ANDERS. Thanks. (*Comes down slowly.*) What're you sore about?

PETREA. Nothing. I ain't sore. You make me sick.

ANDERS (*goes to table downstage left and sits, putting his cap under the chair and fishing in his pocket for a butt*). We finished loading last night—late. Worked the whole bloody night.—Them French shipyards stink. Turn out old wash tubs. Start to list if you spit over the port side. Got no balance to them. Ain't the kind of vessels I'd ship on.

PETREA. If you could ship a'tall—

ANDERS (*gets up and moves over to the counter behind which she is working. Leans over it earnestly*). I could ship if I took a notion to. I'm as good as them Frenchies. —I could ship!

PETREA. Huh! Why don't you, then?

ANDERS. I ain't took the notion, that's all.

PETREA. You tried to ship on the Malmo Ferry, didn't you? What of that?

ANDERS. Aw—

PETREA (*leans over the other side of the counter and talks vehemently into his face*). The Cap'n said, "Anders," he said, "you don't know the difference between port and starboard, fore and aft! Anders," he said, "go home to your Ma and get dry behind the ears!" The Cap'n said that to you—on a ferry-boat!—Huh!

ANDERS. Yah—(*He turns his back to her and leans on the counter.*) Where were you last night, when I was working?

PETREA. Nowhere—

ANDERS. Didn't see nothing of that Vilhelm? (*He turns.*) Did you?

PETREA. No—I went home.

ANDERS. Yah—you went home! (*He comes and sits at the table again. Sulkily.*) You got a lie in your throat! (PETREA *stops washing glasses and looks at him for a short moment. Then she goes out into the kitchen while* ANDERS *lights the cigarette butt he fished out before. She returns with a mug of coffee, swings in behind the counter, and comes out with a bottle of Schnapps and a little thick glass in one hand, the mug*

in the other. She puts the coffee in front of ANDERS,
*pours Schnapps into the small glass, and then tips it
into the coffee.* ANDERS *does not look at her. She
stands for a moment watching him, then she speaks as
she goes back to her glasses.*)

PETREA (*quietly*). I'm knitting a sweater for the Perfes-
sor. That's what I was doing.

ANDERS. You just knit him one!

PETREA. Well, I'm knitting him another. You don't have
to be suspicious and talk to me like that! Anyway,
Villy was out to the lighthouse.

ANDERS. Ah—you knew where he was, didn't you?

PETREA. Sure.

ANDERS. And if he hadn't been to the lighthouse, you
would have been with him, wouldn't you?

PETREA (*turns and looks at him*). Maybe.—How you talk!

ANDERS (*talks partly to her and partly to himself*). I
don't count like them sailors! When they're in town
nobody thinks much of Anders. Dockrat!—That's me!
(*Goes to the window and leans his arms.*) There she
goes—the tanker for Marseilles. (*Sighs and turns back,
leaning on his elbows.*) I'd ship on a big vessel! A white
one—like the Australian one last week. White and shiny
and clean when the sun shone on her, kind of quietlike,
of an afternoon. I'd ship on her and go south with her—
as far south as the ocean runs, I guess! That I would!

PETREA. Huh—!

ANDERS (*goes up and stands behind her*). Petrea?

PETREA. Yah—?

ANDERS. I could do that, couldn't I?—Then it would be well with you and me.

PETREA. Nah—you ain't no sailor, Anders.—Stay-at-home-feller, that's you.

ANDERS. Not like Vilhelm!

PETREA. No—not like him! (*She turns and faces him.*) He can ship on them big vessels. They ain't for the likes of you! He knows how to work with his fists, he does! He can swing them ropes and roar with his big voice! He's a sailing man!

ANDERS (*flatly*). I'm going to kill him for what he done to you!

PETREA (*pause. Then quietly*). I seen him bend an iron bar over his knee.

ANDERS (*returning to the table*). I ain't lived all my life in the docks for nothing. I can take care of myself. (*The door is opened and* HANS *enters, giggling.* HANS *is middle-aged, more or less; a queer mixture of dissipation and sunburned health. He is dirty and unkempt. He is dressed like* ANDERS, *but he is slovenly and unshaven.*)

HANS. Hello—(*He sits on the railing downstage of the door.*) What you two doin'?

ANDERS. Mind your business—. (*He sits.*)

HANS. I was listenin'. Gunnin' for Vilhelm, ain't you?

ANDERS. You heard me.

HANS. Watch it, boy! Villy's a big feller—an' a sailin' man! Heh-heh-heh—wait'll you hear what I know! (*Nobody pays any attention to him.* PETREA *starts to wipe the counter with a wet cloth.*) There's a Tarantula loose in the docks! Heh-heh-heh—I seen it. Yah —I seen it, scurryin' along on its long hairy legs— just as fast as anythin', over behind some crates!

ANDERS (*uninterested*). You don't say?

HANS (*highly amused*). Yah—heh-heh-heh! You don't know what a Tarantula is, do you, Anders? Naw, not bein' a sailin' man yourself, you wouldn't know, would you? We fellers that's been around—we know!

ANDERS (*gets up and starts for him*). I'll fix your stinking tongue for you, that I will!

HANS. No 'fence—no 'fence! It's a spider—bi-i-i-g spider. Yah—(ANDERS *is closing in.*) Get away from me, you Anders!—Know what it does? (ANDERS *has a hold on him now, pulling him off the railing and putting him against the wall by the door. But* HANS *is used to that sort of treatment; he goes right on.*) It bites—right any old place where it can catch a hold!

ANDERS. I'll make you eat your words, you little louse! So I ain't a sailing man?—I'll show you! (*He lets go of* HANS *and turns to* PETREA.) And you, too—and anybody else! (*He turns back to* HANS.) If you could be one—I can! (*He starts back to his chair again.*)

HANS. No 'fence, Anders—

ANDERS (*turns on his way down*). Then what am I?

HANS. A sailin' man, Anders!

ANDERS. All right!—Don't forget it! (*Goes to the table.*)

PETREA. Ain't you the hero!

ANDERS. Shut your lip, woman! (*He sits.*)

PETREA. Huh—don't pay no attention to him, Hans. (*She goes on with her cleaning.*) How about that spider?

HANS. When it bites, you whirl around and around like a bloomin' dervisht right on the spot! And then you die! Just like that, heh-heh-heh, all bloated and blue and nice!

PETREA. Ugh!—What'll you have, Hans?

HANS (*coming down*). Half-coffee, Petrea, with a little ol' Schnapps in it to warm my little ol' gizzard. I ain't the spry talker I used to was.—Can't spin a yarn so good no more.

PETREA. Ain't nothing wrong with your pipes, far as I can see.

HANS. Heh-heh-heh, you don't know nothin', little Petrea. Can I set with you, Anders? (ANDERS *does not answer.*) Thanks to him who offers! (*He sits.*)

ANDERS. Where'd you see that spider, Hans?

HANS. Down by shed thirteen.—Yah, she's 'n unlucky number! Bloody Spaniard unloadin' there.—Cocoa-fibre, wine, blankets, bananas, the devil and his pump-stick! I worked on 'er. Lousy Spaniards wouldn't even gi' me a smoke! Me—what's bummed smokes offa Cap'ns and First Mates! I couldn't even bum a little ol' smoke offen a Spaniard—!

PETREA (*comes with coffee and Schnapps*). You don't wanna get so het up, little Hans. You wanna oil them pipes first.

HANS (*stares up at her*). Heh-heh-heh—
(*He ducks his head and giggles again. When she has finished serving him,* PETREA *turns to go back to the counter. When she goes past* HANS, *he slaps her on the behind. She turns furiously.*)

PETREA. Keep your filthy hands to yourself!—

ANDERS (*rising quickly*). You—!

HANS (*cringing*). I'm sorry—that I am. Ain't nobody ever lets me touch 'em. I like it, same as any other fellow.—

PETREA (*tosses her head and goes back to the counter*). Dirty land-crab—

ANDERS. I'll push that ugly face of yours in yet, you little pig! Keep your hands off my girl, I say to you! Watch it!

HANS. Your girl, little Anders?

ANDERS. Yah!—Any question about it? (*Sitting again.*)

HANS. Nope.—She's a pretty bit of woman, ain't she, Anders?

ANDERS. Maybe she is—and maybe she ain't. Keep your paws to yourself!

HANS. Yah.—(*Confidentially*.) Once I got me a stickin' with a knife for that.

ANDERS. You prob'ly had it coming to you.

HANS. Yah—heh-heh-heh, I sure did that! She sure was a pretty girl, though! That was in Porto Rico! Look.— (*He draws a map on the tablecloth*.) You come up here for the harbor. You don't lay in 'cause of the tide. Then you go ashore through the surf in one of them little canoodles. And there'll be a good stiff breeze will wave them palm trees like anythin'. Then you go up along the waterfront and through this alley here. There's a little bar there. Just a little hole in the wall. That was where she was. Had black hair and black eyes—Gawd, but she was pretty!

PETREA. How you talk, Hans!

HANS. Ain't it the truth!

ANDERS. So what about the sticking?

HANS. I'm comin' to that.—Well, I'm sittin' there, havin' a bit of a drink when she walks by, and I just can't stand the temptin' of it, and then—all of a sudden— this little, swarthy guy is standin' in front of me with blazin' eyes, just as cocky as anythin' and shouting away in some sort of gibberish. I get up, of course, and make for him. He pops a knife out of nowheres—like this—and gives it to me in the arm! Just like that!

ANDERS. Yah?—What'd you do to him?

HANS. Aw—I knock 'im out!—(*He gets up and demonstrates a "one-two."*)—colder'n a fish and get all set to finish him off when the cops come! Then I give them a good dustin' off and beat it back on board!

PETREA. That's some story, that is.

HANS. Yah—I been around. (*He sits again.*) Bloody hell-hole, that same Porto Rico. Them's places you won't never see, little Anders. Ain't foggy and rainy like little Denmark. Hot as blazes down there. Ain't no umbrellas or bicycles either. You walk in the middle of the street and just watch out for the donkeys and the kids, and let the little ol' sun burn the hair right offen your head.—And the women-folks have black eyes! Naw—you won't never see them places!

ANDERS. Shut your mouth! Listen—I got to respect the fact that you've been to sea and that I ain't.—(*He gets up.*) But stop rubbing it in!

HANS (*drinking noisily*). No 'fence—didn't mean no 'fence!

ANDERS. Well, shut it up then—with your talk! I'm going to see them places as well as anybody else! Yah! I'm going to walk in the sun too—and send shawls and amber back to Petrea.—Might even buy her a ring!

PETREA. I got a ring—and a dozen shawls. You wasn't the first, Anders—by a long shot.

ANDERS (*goes toward her by the counter*). No—nor the last neither!

PETREA. I didn't say that.

ANDERS. No, but you meant it—didn't you? (PETREA *does not answer.* VILHELM *appears at the door.*) When I get a'hold of Vilhelm—

VILHELM (*pleasantly*). When you get hold of me, what then?

ANDERS (*looks long at him*). I'll give you something to remember! (*He turns back to the table.*)

VILHELM. I'll thank you for that, Anders. (*He comes inside and goes downstairs. He is tall, heavy, powerful, with an open, honest, pleasant face. He walks and acts like a man with a purpose in life. He is dressed in a short, dark blue mackinaw and dark blue woolen trousers. On his feet are heavy black shoes. When he takes his jacket off, a heavy, dark blue, highnecked sweater is disclosed. He wears an old dark blue yachting cap. His hair is shortclipped.*) Hello, girl! Would you have a kiss for a departing love? (*He kisses her soundly.* ANDERS *turns, making a noise with his chair in his excitement.*) Yes, Anders? (ANDERS *falters, mutters something under his breath, and sits down.*) I'll have Schnapps, Petrea, and a pipeload of that fine tobacco in the special crock.

HANS. So you're settin' sail tonight, hey, Villy?

VILHELM (*coming down to sit with them*). With your permission, Anders. (ANDERS *starts to get up. Ironi-*

cally.) No, don't get up! (ANDERS *sits*.) Yep, tonight's
the night! (*He sits*.)

ANDERS. So you're kissing the girls and smoking the special tobacco. Just like that! Like you was somebody!

VILHELM. Maybe I am, hey, Hans? (*He laughs*. HANS
nods.)

ANDERS. And a joking man, too!

PETREA (*comes down with Schnapps and coffee and the
tobacco crock*). Here, sailor.—Where's your pipe?

VILHELM (*gives her the pipe, at the same time pulling
her down on his lap*). Might as well be comfortable at
your work. Don't give me no coffee, girl! What am I?
An old maid? Just Schnapps to carry away in my belly
out on the ocean. The blasted ocean—ah, how I hate
her, the bloody sea! Like a body'd hate his own Ma!
(*He kisses her*.)

PETREA (*laughing*). I got work to do! Lemme go, you
big ox!

ANDERS. You heard her—she's got work to do!

VILHELM. Sure—so do I. So does everybody, except you.
—You just talk. (*He lets* PETREA *go, getting up, himself,
at the same time*.) Don't go far away, girl. (*He removes his jacket and hangs it over the back of his
chair*.)

PETREA. I ain't going nowhere. (*She returns to her work*.)

VILHELM (*empties his little Schnapps glass. Helps himself again from the bottle that* PETREA *left for him. Sits down again, stretching his legs out and leaning back comfortably, contentedly smoking his pipe*). It's good tobacco, this. Well, lubbers, what's in the wind?

HANS. Nothin', Villy, just nothin'—exceptin' there's a Tarantula loose here somewhere, that's all.

VILHELM. Yah?—where'd that come from?

HANS. Rode in on a Spaniard with a cargo of cocoa-fibre and bananas and that kind o' stuff. And now it's around here somewhere. Maybe it's right in here—who knows? Them's mean things!

VILHELM. Ah—that's nothing. Them spiders couldn't live in this climate—too cold. He'll be dead by now!

HANS. He ain't dead! He's live as a chicken. I seen him hustlin' around—

VILHELM. Nah—he'll die, sure.

ANDERS. What makes you so sure of that?

VILHELM. I've been around.—I've seen them things. They ain't nothing.

ANDERS. Yah—you've been around! I hear you talk all right. With the mouth! And inside your liver is yellow like a quarantine flag. I hear you talk! I hear you say you hate the sea that gives you your bread! A sailing man, ain't you? Scared!—Huh!!

VILHELM. Ah—that's all you know. Wait till your chance comes, and you get out in your first, bloody storm, hey, Hans?

HANS. Yah—he'll have to wait, all right!

VILHELM. And your belly feels like it's filled with sand—slithering, swooshing sand!

ANDERS. What's the matter, sailor? You get seasick?

VILHELM. Sure—sometimes.—Not so much as I used to, but once a year is enough. Them spells you don't forget so easy.

HANS. You sure don't.

VILHELM. And that ain't all!—Wait'll you get your first dose of loneliness out there on a dead sea—a thousand miles or so from land—

ANDERS. Ah—that kind of talk doesn't bother me any. I reckon here'd be one sailor who'd ship for the liking of it, and who'd be that proud of his trade!

PETREA (*coming down*). If you could ship a'tall. Here, you Villy, better drink some coffee with all that Schnapps.

VILHELM. Taking care of me, aren't you, girl? And to-night—you'll come down and see me off? Wave to me and things like that?

PETREA. Sure.—(*Archly.*) And things like that.

ANDERS. She'll be with me tonight, sailor. Won't be any waving. Get a stevie to do it for you.

PETREA. I'll be there, Villy.

HANS (*laughing*). Keep your eyes in your head when you go down, girl. Don't let that spider get you!

VILHELM (*laughing too*). Yah—watch it! An elephant might trample you! (*Draws her to him.*)

ANDERS. Don't be funny! (*Looking at the two.*) You might be walking along the docks, mightn't you, Petrea? And it would be dark, and you couldn't see a thing. Coal-black, excepting around the arc lights. And foggy. And a little beam of light might fall between two big crates. (*Raising his voice, trying to keep them from kissing.*) And there he'd be sitting, waiting for you; little mean eyes looking and looking and long hairy legs tucked up under him all ready to jump on you when you went by! (PETREA *lets go of* VILHELM, *all desire to kiss gone. She starts back towards the counter.* ANDERS *follows.*) And he'd catch you by the leg! Pierce the skin and the flesh with a stinging, smarting pain and hang on! And you wouldn't touch him with your hand—would you? You'd use your handbag, dashing at him, beating and thrashing to get him to let go!

PETREA (*terrified*). Let me alone! Let me alone!

ANDERS. And then you'd get dizzy in your head,—and feel sick and like to vomit, and pretty soon you'd start to sway and turn and twist; and your leg'd swell up and turn blue! And not a soul around to hear you call—or see you whirl!

VILHELM. That's enough of that! Shut up! (*Starts for him.*)

ANDERS. And then you'd fall! Crashing and bumping against the crates! (VILHELM *grabs him.* PETREA *is with her back against the counter.*) And then you'd be dead on the ground!—Dead! (*Straining towards her against* VILHELM's *hold, in a final, hysterical pitch.*) And I'd say good riddance, you little slut!

VILHELM (*hitting him over the mouth, so that he staggers back against the end of the counter*). What's the matter with you? Are you crazy? Don't listen to him, Petrea. That spider's dead a long time ago!

PETREA. Get out of here!—Get him out of here!—He scares me with his filthy tongue!
(ANDERS, *who has been standing against the end of the counter, bolts for the door and is gone.*)

VILHELM (*looking after him*). Phew!—I've seen guys go crazy from hanging to the yardarm in a storm, or from looking at the same dirty faces in the same dirty fo'c'stle too long. But I never saw anything like this!

PETREA. He's been like this ever since I first saw him. I said, "You aren't the first one, Anders, and you won't be the last. I like sailors," I said, "I like 'em too much!" He said, "That's all right. Just give me a little love—as much as you can spare for a guy like me," he said. "I can't afford to be particular."

VILHELM (*turning back*). Beggar!

PETREA. No, it wasn't like that. There was something about him that asked for respect—in a way. And then there was something pitiful—in the way he wanted so bad to be a sailing man. He was kinda nice then, at first. I guess I felt then like I wanted to kinda protect him—to give him a chance to feel strong—and important. But then he got bad and mean and jealous—and everything I did was wrong, and other men weren't supposed to look at me the way they did, or as often as they did.—He tried to cut me up once—with a razor. So I wouldn't be good to look at.—And then he started to call me—well, what he just said! And I ain't, you know that! I just like sailors, that's all. (*She turns back to wiping the counter.*)

VILHELM. I'd better fix him good!

PETREA. No—you want to steer clear of him! He can think of more meanness to do to you when he is mad! Don't have anything to do with him!—Just leave him be!

VILHELM. Then what about you, when I am gone?

PETREA. Ah—I know his tricks. When you're gone, he'll think he has me all to himself—and he'll be just as gentle as a lamb, and make up pretty to me.

VILHELM. That doesn't make me feel any better. I kinda like you, you know that.—I don't want to be out there knowing that you're fooling around with a lunatic and me not able to do anything about it! (*He takes her by the arms and turns her around to face him.*) Look at me.—Lay off him, will you? I'll be back pretty soon. If you gotta fool around, pick somebody nice and harmless. All right?

PETREA. All right, you—Villy. (*She pulls his hair.*) You guys—always so scared your girls'll get in trouble! We

can take care of ourselves.—I'll pick on Hans there, he
can't do any harm.

HANS. Yah—you mean it? (*He starts to get up.*) Say—

VILHELM (*laughing*). Hey—I'm still here! Anyway—you
don't have to pick a corpse for yourself. Somebody
nice and young and gentle and dumb.—Only don't
forget about me!

PETREA. No—I won't forget about you. (*She turns back
to her work.*)

VILHELM (*going back to the table*). Don't get any ideas,
Hans.—(*Slightly threatening.*) Don't get any ideas!—

HANS. Forget it.—I don't have to fool with other guys'
girls. Plenty that want me.—I remember once—(*He
sits.*)

VILHELM. Forget it.—(*Reflectively.*) I don't know. Seems
to me like some guys are made to make a mess out of
things. Ever since I was a little fellow—I knew what
I wanted. I knew where the road was leading. I kinda
knew the meaning of things. I'm going to be a mate
some day—maybe even master of some vessel bound
west or south—or somewhere, and why not? Now, him,
Anders—he's messing around, loading himself down
with a lot of nonsense. He'd never make a sailing man.
He's got no sight of things and—chains—that bind his
feet to the ground. He's not a free man! (*He sits.*) I
feel kinda sorry for him.

HANS. Mebbe the spider upset him. I was tellin' him about
it before you came. We, who've been around, we know

them things and take 'em in our stride—but not him. He got kinda crazy. Well—it might be around here— in the window sill, behind the counter, under the table —somewhere. I don't mean it is—but it might be. Mightn't it?

VILHELM. Ah—forget that spider. It's dead, I tell you. The weather is too cold for it around these parts.
(*A song is heard from offstage.*)

PROFESSOR.

    From Angola to Madeira
    She had sailed the seven seas—

(*The* PROFESSOR *opens the door and enters. He leans over the railing of the steps, holding on with all his might and peering nearsightedly down into the room. He is about sixty, skin and bones. Dressed in a Prince Albert coat, green with age, gray, baggy trousers, tattered shoes and no socks, he presents a grotesque picture with his long hair and beard meticulously well*

*kept. He is bareheaded. He wears a dirty shirt with a
high wing collar around which is tied a shoestring bow
tie. Hanging onto the railing, he continues to sing. His
voice is pleasant, though hoarse from liquor.*)

PROFESSOR.
> She had hit the Riviera
> On a stout Morocco breeze.

PETREA (*smiling up to him*). Go on, Perfesser!

PROFESSOR (*sitting on the top step*).
> And it was like a swan she looked,
> When billowing along;
> And it was like a swan she sang,
> And this'n was her song:
>
> From Angola to Madeira
> I have swayed and shook and skipped,
> And there never was a stormy day
> My topsails weren't dipped!
> And it ain't for my skipper,
> And it ain't for my mate,
> That I ever reached Madeira
> And took on my load of date.

HANS. Ahoy, Perfesser! Heave to and let out the plank!
There's liquor ashore!

PROFESSOR. By the fungi that grow on the subterranean
cliffs!—I smell Schnapps! And though I drink it rarely,
today is a day of celebration for me, so I will take the
greatest of pleasure in joining you! (*He gets up with
some difficulty and maneuvers down to the table, where
he sits.*)

VILHELM. What be you celebrating today, Perfesser?

PROFESSOR. *Are*, little Vilhelm, *are*. "What *are* you celebrating today, Professor?" The rudiments of grammar must never escape your notice! The certain mark of an educated man is not, as some may think, his bright and glaring eye. It is his language—his language, little Vilhelm. *Are* is the word. It is not like you to make mistakes like that.

VILHELM. Ah—a feller slips up now and again.

PROFESSOR. You mustn't—you simply mustn't! (*Simple statement.*) Today is Wednesday.

HANS. Today is Wednesday—right you are.

PROFESSOR. Today is Wednesday—a day of celebration.

HANS. Why?

PROFESSOR. Because it is Wednesday. Isn't that reason enough for you? Tomorrow we must celebrate, because it will be Thursday. A fatiguing, but definitely satisfying reason. Slightly wearying in the long run, but comfortably and easily remembered. Wednesday— a day of feasting; Thursday—a day of feasting, and so on ad infinitum.—Very satisfying!

VILHELM (*laughing*). I don't suppose you ever take a day of rest?

PROFESSOR. A day of rest?—A day of rest is a day of drinking. (*Turns to* PETREA.) Petrea, my child, bring your old Professor a small glass of aquavit, please.

(PETREA *takes* ANDERS' *used glass and wipes it on her apron, then she pours into it from the bottle and pushes it over in front of the* PROFESSOR.)

PETREA. Here—that'll warm you.

PROFESSOR. Yes—that'll warm me.—The medicine of happiness, eh? Happiness—heh, fleeting thing—fluff on the breeze, eh? The sweater was excellent, my dear, and you shall have so many thanks, that you shall.

PETREA. Why, that's nothing, Perfesser. I'll make you a whole batch of 'em, if you want.

PROFESSOR. Ah—I remember—(*He drinks, then holds out his glass for more.*) Please, could I have another glass? (*She pours.*) Thank you.

PETREA (*touching the bottle to his glass*). Health to you, Perfesser.

PROFESSOR. I remember when there were many children in my life. When young eyes still laughed at me every day—and young voices pronounced my name. But now —now I have only you, eh, little Petrea?—Now I have only you—(*Holding up his glass.* ANDERS *appears at the door.*) And this—

ANDERS (*speaking from the door*). And maybe you wouldn't have her so long.—Something might happen to her! (*All turn and look at him. There is a short silence.*)

VILHELM. So you're back again, are you?

ANDERS. Sure—this is a public restaurant. Anybody can come here. (*Pointing at* PETREA.) She says so herself. I got as much right here as you have.

VILHELM. Yah—if you behave yourself.

PETREA. Let him come in. It doesn't matter. He can't do anything.

ANDERS (*coming down*). No—I don't hurt anybody.—You like her, don't you, Perfesser? You wouldn't want to lose her, would you now?—Like me—(*Sits in chair next to* PROFESSOR.)

PROFESSOR. Ah—Anders, you're young. For you there are as many girls as there are molecules in the sea. For me —I'm an old one. For me there aren't any. There used to be the children, but now there's only Petrea left, and whether she's your girl, or Vilhelm's, or somebody else's, I won't lose her—will I, girl?

PETREA. No sir, Perfesser. Don't you listen to that Anders. He ain't right in the head. I'll take what I want in the way of young fellers, and that won't matter one way or another to you and me. (*Gives* ANDERS *a glass and fills it for him.*)

VILHELM. Yah—and what she wants is me. Of course there's a lot of fellers she might take, but I'm the best, ain't I, Petrea? (PETREA *looks at him a while and smiles, nodding.* ANDERS *turns away and goes to the window.*)

HANS. There's a Tarantula loose in the docks, Perfesser.

PROFESSOR. Good Lord! A Tarantula! It'll seek warmth somewhere—I pity the people it visits. I'd like to see it,

never having seen one, except in alcohol; and though
I do not for a moment doubt that it was happy there,
still it was quite dead.

HANS. You don't want to see them alive, Perfesser. They
got a way of biting people to death.

ANDERS (*looking at* VILHELM). 'Specially people they
don't like!

PETREA (*comes down with bottle and fills glasses*). Want
to lay your game of solitaire, Perfesser?

PROFESSOR. No, thank you, child, not today.

PETREA. I just thought you might like to break this up.

PROFESSOR. It's all right, Petrea. Today I'll just talk.

VILHELM (*catching and holding her*). What's the matter,
girl? Can't you stand a little talk of death like that?

PETREA. Not today.

VILHELM (*kisses her*). It's all right, girl. It doesn't apply
to anybody here.

ANDERS (*turns*). Yah?—Why not?

VILHELM. Ah—keep your shirt on!

ANDERS (*stepping towards him*). I'll do that without your
help! (*Coming closer, screwing up his excitement.*)

VILHELM. I told you, you could stay here if you be-
haved yourself! Now watch it! (*He puts a hand against
ANDERS' face and pushes him away.*)

ANDERS (*retreats a few steps and stands indecisively. Then he turns and goes to the window*). I shouldn't ought to have to take those things from you! I ought to kill you!—And I would if—ah, I don't know! (*Looking out of the window.*) Look at all them beautiful vessels! All full of guys like you! (*He turns back. Hysterically.*) Listen—I ain't so bad! I'm just a guy! I got ambitions—want to get somewhere! I just want to be like you fellers, that's all! A sailor like you guys!— Why shouldn't I? What's the matter with me? You guys all stepping on me! There ain't no call for that! I don't hurt nobody!

PETREA (*feels sorry for him. Goes to him*). Come on, Anders. There's nothing wrong with you! Nobody's got anything against you.

ANDERS (*turns away from her*). Leave me alone, will you? (*He sits at another table, brooding.*)

HANS. You're getting jumpier and jumpier every day, you are!
(*He turns back to his drinking and* VILHELM *sits again.* PETREA *returns to their table and fetches the bottle, which she brings to the counter, moving* ANDERS' *glass to where he's sitting as she goes by.* ANDERS *catches her by the wrist.*)

ANDERS. You're *my* girl, ain't you?

PETREA. Now cut it out, will you?

ANDERS (*slinging her arm from him*). You little slut! (*She goes back to the counter.*)

HANS (*to the* PROFESSOR). I was tellin' Anders about that spider. It kinda upset him, didn't it, Anders?
(ANDERS *does not answer.*)

PROFESSOR. Well—we shouldn't have talked about it at all. I should have played my solitaire. Ah—for the good, old peaceful days when the children were there. Then there was laughter. (*Holding up his glass.*) Petrea, please give me more of this, will you?

PETREA. Sure. (*She comes back and pours.* VILHELM *takes hold of her again.*)

VILHELM. I'll be going pretty soon now. God, but you're a nice girl. (*He pulls her down on his lap.*) Be good to me now, before I go, hey? So I'll have something nice to remember.

HANS (*to the* PROFESSOR). I was saying it might be around here. I didn't say it was, but it might be. You said it'd seek warmth somewhere. Well, why not here? I saw it down by shed thirteen, and that ain't far from here.
(ANDERS *looks up at this.* VILHELM *is kissing* PETREA.)

PROFESSOR. Don't let's talk about it any more. (*He drinks.*)

PETREA. I guess, I'll kinda miss you, when you go.

VILHELM. I should hope you would!

PETREA. You'll be gone a good while, I suppose?

VILHELM. I don't know. Mebbe. I'll come back. (*Smiling.*) If a spider or something doesn't get me.

PETREA. Don't be funny. I'll come down tonight.

VILHELM. Wish you could stay with me—and not come back. (*He kisses her again.*)

ANDERS (*makes show of looking under* VILHELM's *chair*). Vilhelm!—I saw something move!—

VILHELM (*without turning*). Hey?—

ANDERS. I saw something move. Under your chair! Hey, Vilhelm! The spider! Under your chair! The spider! It's here!!

VILHELM (*throws* PETREA *out of the way and leaps out of his chair and away*). Where?

ANDERS (*laughs hysterically*). It ain't there! I'm only kidding! That's all! My God, were you scared!

VILHELM. What kind of a joke is that? (*Coming towards him.*) You're going to get what you've had coming to you now!

ANDERS (*getting up slowly*). Can't you take a little joking?

VILHELM. Not from you I can't! (*He grabs* ANDERS *by the front of the shirt.*) All right, you asked for it! (*He pushes* ANDERS *out in the middle of the floor, follows and shoots a couple of blows home, first to his middle, then to his chin.* ANDERS *flies back against the counter,* VILHELM *following, pummeling him. Suddenly a knife is flashing in* ANDERS' *hand.*)

PETREA. Villy! Look out!!
(*But it is too late.* VILHELM *suddenly stops dead in his pummeling of* ANDERS, *lets go a little sound,* "Huh!" *and claws at his middle, as if he had been hit hard. Then he crumples to the floor.* ANDERS *is left standing, holding the knife in his hand. He straightens up.*)

ANDERS. There—I've done it! For once I done what I ought to. Straight and clean like a man! I feel better now. That sort of evens things up.—I guess I won't be a sailing man now.—But it don't matter. It's all right this way.

PETREA (*stunned. Moaning*). Villy! Villy! (ANDERS *looks at her quietly for a moment.*)

ANDERS (*goes towards the door, up the steps. At the top he turns*). I'll be going down to straighten this out. Don't move him. They'll be wanting to see how I did it and how everything is.
(*He goes.* PETREA *starts crying.*)

PROFESSOR (*goes to her*). Here—now—(*She starts for* VILHELM's *body.*) No—don't. Hans, put something over him! (HANS *covers the body with a table-cloth.*) It's queer.—Don't cry. That's the way death comes. Just like that. No use crying. That won't stop anything. Those things just come—and that is that.

CURTAIN

SOUTH AFRICA

BLACK PIET

BY *Robert F. Schenkkan*

THE CHARACTERS

As originally produced under the title of "Boer Commando" by The Carolina Playmakers on their Eighty-second Bill of Experimental Productions of New Plays in the Playmakers Theatre, Chapel Hill, North Carolina, April 28, 1942.

PIET DYCKMA, *"Black Piet,"*
   leader of a Boer Commando ...... Robert Gutknecht
LOUIS, *a young soldier* .... Russell Rogers
JOPIE, *an older soldier* .... Joe Rubenstone
McGOVERN, *an Irish adventurer* .... Robert Carroll
VAN RENSBERG, *a prophet* .... Arthur Persky
AN ENGLISH SOLDIER .... MacCurdy Burnet
GENERAL BOTHA,
   leader of the Boer forces in the Transvaal . Tom Avera

THE SCENE: The top of a kopje, or small hill, in the Transvaal.
THE TIME: Summer, 1902.

THE SCENE

The top of a small kopje, or hill, in the Transvaal. It is night. There is a fire center stage, with some pans and a kettle by it. Boulders are scattered about. A great black-bearded man sits on one up left stage. He is picking rifle cartridges out of a bandolier across his knees and dropping them into a hat beside him. A couple of other bandoliers are piled nearby. Another man lies on a tattered blanket at right stage; he is smoking a pipe. Upstage of him, almost blended into the rock on which he sits, looking down the hill, is a short squat figure. All wear tattered, ragged costumes, part civilian, part military; all are haggard and worn.

continued on next page

63

LOUIS (*singing*).

> My Sari Marais
> Is so far from my heart
> And I'm longing to see her again.
> She lived on a farm
> On the Mooi Rivers bank
> Before I left on this campaign.
> Oh, bring me back to the old Transvaal;
> That's where I long to be.
> Way yonder 'mongst the mealies
> By the green thorny tree
> Sari is waiting for me.
> I wonder if I'll ever see
> That green thorny tree
> There where she's waiting for me.

(*He breaks off suddenly and sobs, bowing his head. The black-bearded man looks up at him. The short man on the rock up right stands suddenly, crosses abruptly to the boy. He seems about to speak, but instead, as the younger man gestures pleadingly, slaps him hard across the mouth with the back of his hand. The man on the blanket rises in remonstrance. He is cowed by a look. The short man, PIET, goes back towards the rock. Suddenly a horse whinnies off to the left. Everyone looks in the direction of the sound. Two other horses contribute to the eerie noise.*)

PIET. (PIET DYCKMA [1] *is a short, squat, fierce-looking man of forty. At rest he is as motionless as rock. When he moves, it is powerfully, decisively. His whole heart is in the war. This is his commando*). The horses, Louis. (*Without a word,* LOUIS *picks up a rifle and goes out left.*)

MAC (*a frank-faced Irishman, hearty, simple. He fights because he likes it. About thirty years old*). The lad wasn't meanin' anythin', Piet.

PIET. No one gives up. No one; remember that. Botha [2] would not give up. We will not. (*He goes back to his rock.*)

MAC. You're pretty rough on the lad, considerin'—today.

JOPIE (*an enormous, lumbering, black-veldt Boer*). And that wasn't all, Mac. The British are in Salverdam. The messenger to Botha told him.

MAC. Salverdam! But that's your district, too, Jopie. [3]

JOPIE. Ja.

MAC (*after a pause*). They'll have put your family—in a camp?

JOPIE (*only a break in the rhythm of his work gives any clue to his emotion*). I suppose.

MAC. Ahhh, this bloody war! I'm sick of it.

1. Pronounced Pēēt Dīk'ma.
2. Pronounced Boh'tah.
3. Pronounced Yŏ'pee.

JOPIE. You, Mac?

MAC. I know, I could be quittin' any time, couldn't I? I haven't got anythin' to lose. (*Calling out.*) D'ye hear me, Black Piet?

PIET. I hear you. You do not mean it. If you did— (*He pats the revolver at his side.*) And you had better be quiet, anyway. It is not good.

MAC. Ahh, you're a tough one, bejasus. How you've held us together through all this, the starvin' and freezin' and runnin', I don't know. But I'm sick of it now, Piet. I've had enough. I'd give me right hand for a square meal, I'm that hungry. And look at us. We're no army. We're a bunch of human scarecrows. We'd 've quit if we hadn't won this scrap today.

PIET (*with quiet confidence*). I know. That's why we fought. Finding Botha on the other side of the kopje [1] was luck.

MAC. Well, it's not luck enough. His men are starvin' too. And all we got from these damned Englishmen was a package of tea!

JOPIE. And cartridges.

MAC. And it cost us Paul.

PIET (*pointing out towards the enemy*). Mac. Look down there. Look at them down there. The fires on the plain. Our own at the foot of the kopje are nothing. Fifty

1. Pronounced cup'ya.

men. But there's three thousand. All Botha's army. And their fires—pinpricks of light in Afrika—but every one a torch—to burn the khakis.[1]

MAC (*goes towards him, and as he reaches the edge of the kopje, speaks*). God, but this is a big country. Y' could drop Ireland in this one plain and she'd be swallowed up.

PIET (*with growing intensity*). Ireland! They call it an emerald, don't they? A little green stone. But Afrika, Afrika's a black thunderhead standing over you, and you a little man on a pebble in a small bit of time. Like a piece of this dirt in space. Aaah, you'll never know her, McGovern; you'll never strike your roots into her. There she is, stretched out in front of me, not for you and the other uitlanders, but for me and mine. You can never stand here and say, this is my country. (*He shrinks back into himself and is silent.*)

MAC (*shakes his head*). I don't want to neither. Ah, it's all right, but hell, it's too damned big, too empty, too much sky. (*He shrugs off the rest.*) Seems to be a lot of movin' around in Botha's camp. Could that messenger 've brought word of a new campaign with De Wet [2] in the east? Maybe he needs us up there.

PIET (*sharply*). De Wet needs no help.

MAC. Maybe not, but I'll bet he could use us just the same. Or Botha, anyway, the fox. Why, I'm thinkin' he must have some Irish blood in him to be the fighter

1. The British, because they wore khaki uniforms.
2. Pronounced Da Vět.

that he is. Sure now, with a dozen like him we'd a licked the British long ago. Don't ye think so, y' ould atheist? (*Having crossed to* JOPIE, *he slaps him on the shoulder.* JOPIE *looks up at him.* MAC *retreats.*) All right. All right. Y' needn't be so loquacious about it. Talkin' to you Dutchmen is like talkin' to a stone wall. And it's no wonder, with this damned language o' yours. I can hardly talk meself. (*He sits again.*) But ye're an ould atheist, just the same. How a good Irish Catholic like meself ever come to be mixed up with you Calvins is more than I can ever tell. (*Lying down.*) Call me whin tea's ready. Ahh, but it's good to be lyin' down.

JOPIE (*with a gleam of humor*). Alive, you mean.

MAC (*laughing*). You never said a truer word. Y' know, one o' them divils took the damned hat right off me head. Lord Vivian's hat that I been wearin' since Spion Kop.[1]

JOPIE. You can get a new one. A lot lying around after today.

MAC (*fondling it*). No, I'll stick to the ould one. This skull and crossbones is me lucky charm. (*Looking at the label inside.*) Lord Vivian Grey, Vth Queen's Rifles. Y' know, when I shot it off him on that last charge, that English bastard smiled at me, 'fore he rode away. I swear he did. *You* been able to get a pair o' boots, yet?

JOPIE. These Tommies were all too small.

1. Pronounced Spee'en Kup".

MAC. Put up a pretty good scrap, though. For khakis. Y' know, I think they're gettin' tougher.

JOPIE. They take cover better.

MAC. Remember Magersfontein?[1] Like shootin' snipe. Today was different. Real comfortable place we took, though. Without the bodies. Did you get 'em all buried, Piet?

PIET. They've buried everyone we could find. Ought to have let them rot on the ground, the swine.

MAC. We wouldn't be able to stay here long if we did. You've smelled 3-day Englishmen; they ain't good.

PIET. It's good to hear a spade full of dirt thump down on a khaki corpse. Aaaah, I hate them; even when they're dead and can't lord it over us any more, I hate them.

MAC (*after a pause*). How long we goin' to wait for the Lion this time, friend jackal?

PIET. You ask too many questions, McGovern.

MAC (*after another pause*). I like to listen to the dulcet tones of me own voice, little Piet. Perhaps you'd care to join me in a confab about the moon and the stars? (*Piet crosses over to* JOPIE.) No? Oh, hum. (*He lies down again.*)

PIET (*looking at the bullets*). Is that the lot? (JOPIE *nods;* PIET *shakes his head.*) Not enough.

1. Pronounced Ma'gerss-fun-tine".

MAC. Not enough for killin', Piet? Ye'd kill the Lord God himself if he came to y' in a British uniform, wouldn't ye?

PIET. God never saw a British uniform.

MAC (*mocking*). This must be the devil's year surely. We haven't done so damned good. Maybe we ought to quit, eh, Piet?

PIET. Never. Not while an Englishman walks between Capetown and Pretoria.

MAC (*taunting*). Think you can kill 'em all? All the thousands and thousands of 'em?

JOPIE. Careful, Mac.

PIET (*oblivious*). They will get tired of this. That detachment we cut up today. They lost thirty men. We lost only five.

MAC (*serious now*). But it's that they're wearin' us down, Piet. The blockhouse system is ruining us. They can lose ten men to our one.

PIET (*flaming*). Are you getting ready to give up, too? Like the boy?

MAC. We'll all have to be doin' that. It only stands to reason we'll have to quit...

PIET. You quit, you vervlukte [1] Irishman. You ought to give up. Go back where your English friends can tell you what to do. Back to Ireland!

1. Damned.

MAC (*rising*). Take it aisy, Piet darlin'. Don't get me angry or I'll break your little Dutch neck for ye.

PIET. Paul's death has frightened you, too, hei?

MAC. Dyckma, I haven't starved and froze and burned and damned near died in your lousy country for nothin'. I've done my share for the Afrikanders.

PIET. We don't owe you anything, Mac. Remember Ardaskap.[1] You're still alive.

MAC. That wasn't me you saved; it was just another man to fight the British. Y' don't do anythin' but for that. You haven't got a heart inside y' at all, just one big black gut full of hate.

PIET (*savagely exultant*). Hate? God, yes. But here's something else, McGovern, something you don't know anything about. Maybe you could call it love, hei? For Afrika and for my people. We settled this country. We fought off the savages. We created a free republic here. And we're going to keep it. No matter what happens we are going to keep on fighting. No one and nothing can stop us. Don't get in our way, McGovern. Don't get in our way! (MAC *has fallen back before his vehemence.* JOPIE *has gotten up.* PIET *pulls himself together.*) Keep on with those cartridges, Jopie. I'm going down to look after the rest of the men. (*He goes out right.*)

MAC. What the hell's the matter with me? Why didn't I... (*He takes a step right.*)

1. Pronounced Ar'dus-kap".

JOPIE. You are afraid of him, Mac.

MAC. Ah, hell, the man ain't born I'm afraid of. It's just . . .

JOPIE. We all are, Mac. And you don't understand Piet.

MAC. Neither do you. How the hell can you? How can anybody?

JOPIE. Ja—en nee.[1]

MAC. You don't know what he means when he goes off his nut like he did before, talking about this god-damned emptiness like it was a woman. (*He laughs.*) Africa for the Afrikander gets a new slant.

JOPIE. Ja—he means Afrika for the Afrikander—and yet something else, too.

MAC. Yeah, but what is it? Now if it was fightin'. Y' get somethin' outa fightin'. I don't know exactly . . . (*Re-living the moment.*) Remember Magersfontein? Lyin' behind that rock, waitin', watchin' them deploy in front of y'. An' then they come. Chargin' up the hill, the horses strainin', the khakis knee to knee. Y' see him, your man. Get the sights on him. Crack! The rifle butt grinds into your shoulder and y' smell that sharp smell, an' he topples slowly, and the horse turns and runs. All around y' the spurts of flame and the high whistle of the bullets and the yells—and the khakis break and run. That three times and it's over. It's get-tin' dark. Y' come out stiff and tired. An' satisfied. That's what it is.

1. Pronounced Yah n ney: yes and no.

JOPIE. No. Fighting is not that. Not for me. (*With an effort.*) I have never spoken of this. But I remember you then. Sitting eating your biltong.[1] Lighting a match for your pipe on that dead Lancer's boot. Agh!

MAC. If it isn't that, it's nothin'.

JOPIE. It is my duty—God demands this of me.

MAC. Piet's too?

JOPIE. Ja, ja but... (*He makes a despairing gesture.*) I fight to keep Kitchener from my own stoep—even now when it is too late. We must. I go on fighting for that. Piet, too. And yet... for Afrika? For the Boers?

MAC. He's hard. He's got this idea—or it's got him—and it'll ride him to a fall sure.

JOPIE. The things he says, though. I feel them, too, in a way. But it is not that for me. It is the other.

MAC. Nice. You havin' somethin' to fight *for*. Me, I just fight. Like the dumb Mick I am. For the kick of it. The ridin', the shootin', for this. Even the starvin'. It's right this way. It's livin'. Until I get the one's got my name on it. It'll come singin', "McGovern, McGovern"— and that'll be it. (*He crosses himself.*) That'll be the end o' me.

JOPIE. One thing Piet means you can see. There, in Kimberley, in the diamond mines the English have been. And with them people, people. Too many people here already.

---

1. Pronounced bill'tŏng: dried meat, eaten raw.

MAC. Too many people! Mither o' saints if that ain't a laugh. There ain't a human bein' to a square mile—ceptin' bushmen, and they ain't human.

JOPIE (*going back to his former seat. He picks up a cartridge and cuts the soft lead of the tip into quadrants with his hunting knife*). And Englesche.[1]

MAC. Yeah, and the English. There'll be less o' them, too, when we start usin' those.

JOPIE. Piet says we don't have cartridges enough otherwise.

MAC. Y' know, one o' them Fusiliers had five bullets in him, and still kickin'.

JOPIE. Not these.

MAC (*laughing*). Bejasus, that's no lie. In like a pin and out like a plate, eh, Jopie? (*Seriously.*) But the general ain't goin' to like us usin' those. Y' know what he's always sayin' about the damned rules.

JOPIE (*shrugs*). It is for Piet to say.

MAC. Wonder what it's like to get one o' them in yer gut. If that Lancer had used one at Ardaskap, I wouldn't be walkin' around no more.

JOPIE. God has watched over you.

MAC (*looks at* JOPIE, *starts to speak, changes his mind.* LOUIS *returns quietly*). Evenin', young feller, how're the horses?

1. Pronounced Eng'al-ssa.

Louis. Nothing the matter.

Mac. Sure took you long enough.

Louis (*to* Jopie). Making dum-dums? Let me help. (*He sits by* Jopie *and taking out his knife begins to notch cartridges also.*)

Mac. Ain't everybody sociable, though.

Louis. Ah, still! Hold your mouth, McGovern.
(*There is a silence. A voice is heard singing a Calvinist hymn.*)

Mac. O Mither o' God, it's Van Rensburg! [1]
(Van Rensburg *enters. He is a man nearing sixty, tall, lean, his eyes alight with the fire of fanaticism.*)

Mac. Top o' the evenin' to y', Jeremiah.

Van Rensburg. Ah, it's the unbeliever again. Why do you remain among the chosen people, son of Belial?

Mac. I been doin' a little fightin', remember?

Louis (*sharply*). Let him alone, Mac.

Van Rensburg. Poor Louis. Do not grieve for your own. Remember the word of the Lord. Be not dismayed.

Louis. I'm all right.

Van Rensburg. Your brother fought for the Lord, Louis. He shall not die. (*The horses whinny again off to the left. Everyone stops dead.*)

1. Pronounced Fun Renss'berg.

MAC. This time I'll go meself. (*He picks up his rifle and starts out.*) They ain't doin' that for fun.

LOUIS (*to the others*). I looked. There was nothing.

JOPIE. You want to be sure, Louis. Without a horse here, a man's as good as dead.

LOUIS. I know that; I'm no child.

VAN RENSBURG. We will be saved, Jopie. We have a task.

LOUIS (*bitterly*). We have a task! We have a task! That's what's making us live out on the veldt, while they burn our homes and imprison our people. That's what killed Paul. We never should have listened to you. Because we can't win. We can't. We're starving. (*Everyone looks away but* VAN RENSBURG.) You all know it. Those Englishmen we killed. They were well-fed. They were clean. They had decent clothes. I tell you I nearly cried when I saw them lying there. I'm not ashamed of it. I envied them.

VAN RENSBURG. Louis. Louis. You must be brave.

LOUIS. Don't talk to me. Don't try to quiet me. Kitchener is in Salverdam, Van Rensburg, in my own district. Is that God's will?

VAN RENSBURG. Remember what I have told you, my boy. All they that were—

LOUIS. Ahhh, what do you know? We can't kill them all. They're like locusts. Eating everything that's green, blackening the whole earth. What if we cut up a company of Fusiliers today? Tomorrow they recruit three more to send against us. England is an empire of millions. How can we hope to stand against them? (*He sees* PIET, *who has entered in the middle of this speech, and falters.*) I ... I didn't know you were there.

PIET. What do you want to do now, Louis?

LOUIS. I ...

PIET. Well?

LOUIS (*with sudden determination*). I want to go home. I want to get out of here and live like a human being instead of a hunted animal. I want to eat decent food and sleep in a bed. (*Boldly.*) And that's what I'm going to do. I'm going to saddle up and get out of this place.

PIET (*drawing his pistol*). Stay where you are, Louis.

JOPIE. Piet!

PIET. Be quiet, Jopie. You only fought because of your brother, didn't you, Louis? Because of Paul.

LOUIS. No, I didn't, and if I did, what of it? No one here was a better soldier. No one could handle a horse better. Yes, part of the reason I rode was Paul. And now he's dead. (*Screaming.*) And I've had enough. I can't stand any more. Piet, please, please. For God's sake, let me go home. I can't keep on. I can't—I can't—(*He has fallen to his knees.*)

PIET (*pushes him down*). You will stay. Even with soldiers like you, I will beat them yet. (*He puts his gun away.*)

MAC (*appears with an English soldier, whom he is half-supporting; the man has been wounded in the leg and the head and looks like a blood-stained ghost*). Look! I found us some company for tay. (*He places* THE TOMMY, *who seems afraid as well as wounded, against a boulder down left and goes to the fire.*) He got wounded, lay in that gully down there, and tried to catch him a horse after it got dark—but the horses caught him. (*Laughing.*) He thinks we're goin' to eat him. It's all right, me boy, we're not cannibals. That is, only ould Piet over there.

PIET. Don't joke, McGovern. So we've got a live Englishman, have we? (*He crosses to* THE TOMMY.) Surprised we can talk your pig language, hei? And frightened, too, are you not? Answer me.

THE TOMMY. No.

PIET. You lying pig! You've heard what we do to you when we capture you, have you not? Your lying English newspapers tell you. So that you'll come over here and take our country from us.

MAC. Lay off him, Piet.

PIET. What do you want here? Why do you come? The thousands and thousands of you. Why don't you stay at home and leave us in peace?

VAN RENSBURG. God shall avenge us, Englishman.

THE TOMMY. D'ye think we want to come 'ere to this bloomin' desert? God, there ain't even any people 'ere. In Lunnon a chap ...

Piet. In London! Why don't you stay there then?

The Tommy. You 'aven't treated Englishmen the way they ought to be treated.

Piet. That's a lie! We've treated you better than you deserve. What do you know of it?

The Tommy (*valiantly*). You kept us from 'avin' the right to vote, didn't you?

Piet. The right to vote. The right to vote. Can I vote in England? You little fool! (*Contemptuously*.) These are the rulers of the world. ·

The Tommy. That's right. And we're goin' to rule South Africa before we're through.

Piet (*vehemently*). You will. You shall think so. But you never will. Kitchener will have to kill every Afrikander first. We can outride you and outshoot you. We have for three years and we can keep on doing so.

Mac. Sure you're goin' to talk him to death, ain't you?

Piet (*turning*). Take care, McGovern.

Mac (*coming down to him*). The lad's hurt, Piet.

Piet. Someday you will go too far.
(*There is a momentary pause, then* Mac *turns to* The Tommy.)

Mac. How about some tea, son?

THE TOMMY. Thanks.
(*There is a sound of horses' hooves below to the right.*)

MAC (*simultaneously with the off-stage sound*). Don't thank me, it's yours.

LOUIS. What's that?

JOPIE. Someone will have ridden over from Botha's camp, I think.

MAC (*turning back*). Y' see, we wouldn't have had it, if we hadn't taken it away from you. Usually we don't have any. Look at him, Jopie. That's London's idea of a *Dublin* Fusilier. Niver saw the ould sod in his life. Am I right, me boy? (THE TOMMY *nods again, smiling a little now.*) Well, here you are. (MAC *goes towards the soldier to give him a tin cup full of tea.*) We'll have a toast, shall we? (*He winks towards* PIET *who is turned away.*) To the King Emperor. (*He holds up the cup, then hands it to* THE TOMMY. LOUIS *gasps, clenches his fist.*)

JOPIE (*coming down between* PIET *and* MAC). Mac!

THE TOMMY (*has been clutching the cup, and has struggled half to his feet, leaning for support upon the boulder behind*). 'Is Majesty, the King!
(PIET *pushes* JOPIE *aside easily; he is half-mad with rage.*)

PIET. Ah, you pig, you khaki pig. (*He snatches the cup.*) I'll toast your King! (*He dashes the contents of the cup in* THE TOMMY'S *face, and then turns upon* MAC.) And you, you Irish bastard. In your heart you still

wear the Cross of St. George. I warned you, by God!
(*As he draws his pistol,* Louis *springs forward and grasps his arm.* Piet *sends him sprawling.* Mac *grabs for a rifle lying nearby but is prevented from reaching it by* Jopie. *At this moment,* General Botha *strides on stage. An intellectual, a lawyer in private life, he has demonstrated his ability as a leader by rising to supreme command of the Boer forces. He is comparatively young, in his middle thirties.*)

Botha (*a plain greeting. No one salutes*). Mijnheeren.[1]

Louis. General Botha!

Jopie. General.

Piet (*the two men have not moved*). Later, McGovern.

Mac (*turning*). Top o' the avenin' to ye, Gineral.

Botha. Good evening, Black Piet.

Piet. Good evening, General Botha.

Botha. I understand you had a pretty warm engagement today.

Mac. It'll do.

Botha. Did you lose heavily?

Louis. No, not heavily. (*He turns upstage and sits looking out over the hill.*)
(*There is a silence.* Botha *sees* The Tommy.)

1. Pronounced min-hair'en: gentlemen.

BOTHA. Ah, took a prisoner, I see.

MAC. Well—we found him.

PIET. What is it, General? Do you want to see me alone?

BOTHA (*surprised*). Has that been the Boer custom, Dyckma? We have nothing to hide. Well, what I have to say will interest all of you—particularly our guest here. (*Gesturing towards* THE TOMMY.)

VAN RENSBURG. Let Israel's sons not welcome their foemen. For God has set His seal upon their destruction.

BOTHA. Ah, good evening, Van Rensburg. Your prophecies—well. (*Turning to* THE TOMMY.) How do you like South Africa?

THE TOMMY. It wasn't s' bad—till I got these presents. (*Gestures toward his wounds.*)
(*Everyone laughs but* PIET.)

BOTHA (*heavily*). Well, you'll be going home soon.

MAC. Yeah, we can't use anythin' but your uniform. Think *his* boots'll fit you, Jopie?

PIET. You still insist we send them back, General?

BOTHA. What would you do, Piet? We have no place to keep them.

PIET. One bullet now would save a good many later on.

BOTHA. You're a trifle savage, Dyckma.

PIET. And you're too civilized. You always have been. This is war.

BOTHA (*angrily*). We're not Zulus, Dyckma. That's one reason why ... well, let's not discuss that now. What I have come to ... (*As he turns to sit in* JOPIE's *former place, he sees the bullets* JOPIE *has been working on.*) What's this! Dum-dums? (*Silence.*) Your orders, Black Piet?

PIET. Why not?

BOTHA (*frowning*). It's against the laws of war.

PIET. The British have used them.

BOTHA. And no one has criticized them more severely than their own people. This is one more reason why the war must come to an end. We are a civilized and cultured people, Dyckma. This sort of thing will blacken our name forever.

PIET. To an end, did you say?
(*Everyone moves towards* BOTHA.)

BOTHA (*pauses*). Yes, that's what I have come to tell you. I'm riding out to all the free commandos around my camp. I wanted to tell you myself. Kitchener has offered us the same terms as a year ago. We must ... (*With a helpless gesture.*) It is over.

LOUIS (*slowly, unbelievingly*). Over. That means we can go home?

MAC. It—it can't be.

VAN RENSBURG. That cannot be. The Lord has said our enemies shall be destroyed. I have seen it, I myself, written in letters of fire upon the heavens.

BOTHA. That messenger you sent on to me this morning brought me De Wet's agreement that we should treat with the British. The chief burghers are to meet at Vereeniging to decide.

MAC. After three years. It doesn't seem possible.

VAN RENSBURG (*leaps upon a boulder*). It shall not come to pass that Israel be deserted by the Lord, his God. Despair not in this hour of darkness, children of Israel. Pray! Pray God open the heavens and pour out his wrath upon our enemies! I say to you they *shall* be confounded! It is God's will.

LOUIS (*angrily*). Why, why did it have to be today? Why at the end of the fighting? Answer me that, Van Rensburg! You're God's spokesman, answer me that. (*In a whisper.*) Oh, Paul, Paul.

PIET (*slowly*). Not you and De Wet—I don't believe it.

BOTHA. I'm going tomorrow. You may join me if you wish. (PIET *looks at him.*) Though we know what must be decided.

PIET. Never! Never! I will not make peace with them— if I have to fight them with my bare hands and alone. I will never surrender.

BOTHA. There is no choice.

PIET (*pleading*). But we're not beaten, Botha. We win out over them every time we meet. Look at *our* commando today ...

BOTHA. No, we're not beaten in that sense. We still have an army in the field. But we can't go on.

PIET. Why not? Why not? We're fighting for our lives. Too many of us have given our lives to stop now.

BOTHA (*sharply*). Dyckma, I tell you we can't go on. The war is lost. We refused their peace offer before, hoping for a miracle. It has not happened. The blockhouse system is catching the commandos like rats in a trap. Here in the north we're broken. They have our capital.

PIET. If you make peace, they'll take everything, too. Our whole country, our souls ...

BOTHA. The peace will be just. The same terms offered me a year ago.

PIET (*with bitterness*). Justice? How can one expect justice from the khakis? Look at the way they've worked in the Transvaal. They hate us; they want to destroy us. What is left of our homes now but the blackened stoeps?

BOTHA. You're wrong, Dyckma. The terms are generous and we can expect justice from the English—in time. Their own people have decried the blockhouse system, called it "methods of barbarism." That's what—

PIET. And so they are!

THE TOMMY. You'll get a fair deal.

PIET. Hold your mouth, you khaki swine!

MAC. Yeah, the bloody English. There's always a *few* that sees the right.

VAN RENSBURG. We shall not be delivered into their hands.

PIET. You, Botha, what do you know of it? You're a University man, a city man still. When I was born, the nearest other farmhouse was Jopie's. You couldn't see the smoke of it. Nothing but the veldt. The sky and the plain. We lived alone, as men ought to live. We depended on no one. We were free. When the English came we picked up our rifles and rode out, as our fathers did in '81. We've been at Magersfontein, Colenso,[1] Ladysmith, Ardaskap. Our dead are buried there. We have fought for three years as no other people in the world could have done—a handful against millions. And now you ask us to stop. You say we must stop because we cannot win. Because we are starving and ragged. How can we stop? How can we make peace with them, while a cell in our bodies can still fight on? *You* make peace. I will go on as before.

BOTHA. Ah, Dyckma, when you're beaten, you're beaten. What have we to gain by more bloodshed? Nothing. What are we fighting for? Our homes? We could never go home again. For a free South Africa? We'd have no hand in shaping it. We'd be outlaws, Piet, outlaws. Hunted as we are now, but with no hope left.

1. Pronounced Ka-lĕn'sō.

JOPIE. He is right, Piet. It is over, finished.

BOTHA. We fought. Good. We had to fight. It was an historical necessity. The British had to fight. Maybe it could have been avoided; the point is, it wasn't. Now we have fought—and we have lost. Shall we commit national suicide? Give them our country entirely? If we make peace, we may have something to say; if we go on fighting, they will take everything. We will be disinherited.

PIET (*almost piteously*). You don't understand. You don't understand. None of you.

BOTHA. Perhaps this war has been God's punishment upon us for our sins. Well, we have paid our due in blood. The sacrifice is over.

PIET (*bitterly*). And who will punish Engeland? Or has she not sinned?

BOTHA. God will punish England—in His time. They will pay, too, in blood. There is justice. No one escapes. No one. No nation does evil but is chastised. No nation fails its responsibility but someday it must pay ... And yet you will see, these people will be just. Today's few will be tomorrow's many. We can make peace with them. They will be just.

THE TOMMY. Good for you, guv'nor. That's tellin' 'im. (*There is an awkward pause.*)

BOTHA. Well, that's it. I'll ride back. You can keep your commando in the field—if they want to stay. It will make a bargaining point, perhaps. I'll take your prisoner across the lines. (*To* MAC.) Will you help him down the kopje? I'm sorry. Good night. (*He goes off right.*)

MAC. I think I'll go along with the Gineral. Take care o' sonny here. I'll come round the kopje for the horses. You stayin', Jopie? Louis?

JOPIE. Maybe Louis and I will ride part way with you. We'll go home soon.

LOUIS. Yes. That's what I want to do.

MAC. Piet? (*There is a pause.* MAC *starts folding his blanket.*) I'll be goin'. (*Pause.*) Good thing a man travels light. (*Crosses and helps* THE TOMMY *up. They start to the right. As* THE TOMMY *passes* PIET *their eyes meet. Hatred like a spasm of pain convulses the Boer leader.* THE TOMMY *shrinks.*) Good-bye.

LOUIS. We'd better hurry, Jopie.

JOPIE. Ja. (*He makes a futile gesture towards* PIET.) Good-bye, Piet.

LOUIS. Good-bye.
(*They go out.*)

VAN RENSBURG (*coming towards him*). Be not dismayed, Piet Dyckma . . . (PIET *turns upon* VAN RENSBURG *as if about to speak, angrily. Then, all his blind rage welling up within him, he strikes the old man violently across the chest with the back of his arm.* VAN RENSBURG, *hurled to the ground, rises and hobbles off right.* PIET, *after the blow, crosses up and faces off to the rear. He stands rigid, his fists still clenched. He begins to sob.*)

CURTAIN

SYRIA
FLEAS AND FIGS
BY *Mary-Averett Seelye*

THE CHARACTERS

As originally produced by The Carolina Playmakers on their Eighty-eighth Bill of Experimental Productions of New Plays in the Playmakers Theatre, Chapel Hill, North Carolina, March 25, 1943.

HESTA .... Kitty Lee
FAREEDEH .... Phyllis Parker
MARIA .... Louise Platt
AAZAM .... Peter Strader
SELIM .... Bill Pitts

THE SCENE: A courtyard of a village house in the Lebanon Mountains.

THE TIME: A morning in late summer.

THE SCENE

The stage is divided into three levels, each about a foot high, graduating from downstage left to upstage right. (These are referred to as steps in the directions of the play.)

The scene is a walled courtyard in front of a two-story house, on a hot sunny day. The wall is about seven feet high, made of large bricks of sandstone. In the wall at the left is the door into the street, and, just above this, the wall juts into the courtyard a bit and extends on upstage. In the back wall, right of center, is a small round-topped door leading out onto the hill. One side of the house is seen, set diagonally upstage right, and its surface is dirty plaster. There are two windows on the second floor with blinds closed and one large open window on the first floor, a foot off the ground. In the downstage wall of the house, disappearing off stage, is a door, with a small basket lying on the ground to its left. Below this, on the second level, is a small, low bench on which FAREEDEH *is sitting, pounding meat in the stone mortar in front of her. To her right, on the third level, rests a large round platter of dry lentils. She is making "kibbeh."* [1]

FAREEDEH *is in her thirties, well-preserved, and physically strong. Her face shows her to be the type that thrives on hard work. She has been pounding the kibbeh*

1. A common meat dish in Syria. Part of the preparation involves pounding the meat in a stone mortar with a wooden pestle.

a long time, and sighs and groans and God's name are heard every now and then. From inside the house is heard singing in a high, nasal voice. It is HESTA'S *voice. She is lying on a mat near the window, unseen by the audience.*

HESTA'S VOICE. Fareedeh!

FAREEDEH. What do you want?

HESTA'S VOICE. Fareedeh!

FAREEDEH. What do you want!?

HESTA'S VOICE (*laughing*). You should see the baby!

FAREEDEH (*stops her pounding*). What's he doing? (HESTA'S *voice is heard laughing.*) What's he doing?

HESTA'S VOICE. Sleeping.

FAREEDEH (*under her breath*). Y'Allah! (*Shouts back.*) That's a miracle.
(HESTA *continues singing and* FAREEDEH *mumbles sounds as she pounds.*)

FAREEDEH (*grumbling to herself*). Why should I care, anyway? If she's lazy, she's lazy. So what do you care? So I have to do all the work!

MARIA (*from the street outside*). Fareedeh!

FAREEDEH (*stops pounding*). Maria! (*Recognizing the voice, she rushes to meet* MARIA *at the door to the street. The latter is in her early twenties—and thin. Her pallidness shows up her wondering eyes and natu-*

rally credulous expression. When she enters, she is greeted by FAREEDEH *with much hugging and kissing on each cheek alternately.*) How nice you're back. How's Najla? How's your brother-in-law? How're the children?

MARIA. Thank goodness they're all well now. Najla sent you her love. And you? How've you been?

FAREEDEH. Well, thank you. Come in. Come in. (*They go over to the right,* MARIA *sitting on the step and* FAREEDEH *back on her bench.*) My, it's nice to see you again!

MARIA. It's nice to be back! They tell me Hesta had a boy this week.

FAREEDEH (*beaming*). Ah, 'Smallah, may he be preserved.

MARIA. He's still alive?

FAREEDEH (*taking up the pestle*). Yes.

MARIA. Yeeee! How fortunate.

FAREEDEH. Well, it's about time after three babies. (*She starts pounding.*)

MARIA. Yes, but the others were girls.

FAREEDEH (*stops pounding*). Girls or no girls, she should do better than to sleep on top of them.

MARIA. How can she help it? She's so fat, and when you sleep, your head sleeps too.

FAREEDEH. Look at Salma. She's beautifully fat, but does she sleep on her babies? No.

MARIA. Poor Hesta. But now Allah's brought her a son. He wouldn't do that for nothing. Tell me, how is she? Why isn't she out here helping you?

FAREEDEH (*pounding again*). Ach, you know Hesta. She's so lazy, she sleeps all day and all night—except when she eats.

MARIA. So you must fix all the food? (FAREEDEH *shrugs her shoulders.*) She should be ashamed of herself not helping you at all. And why are you making kibbeh?

FAREEDEH. Tomorrow's the seventh day after the baby came, and Aazam wants plenty of food for all the guests. (*She stops pounding.*) Ach, you should see Aazam! He acts as if this were the first boy ever born in the world. "Fareedeh," he says, "you must do everything right. Allah didn't send us a son for nothing. The other babies died because they were girls. This one he meant especially for me—to carry on my name." (*She laughs. Baby's cries are heard.*) Maria, look in the window and see if the baby's all right with her.
(MARIA *gets up and goes over to look and signals* FAREEDEH *to come. The latter goes over and they smile as they look in,* MARIA *upstage of* FAREEDEH. *At that moment* AAZAM *comes in from the street at the left. He is a spindly fellow of medium height with reddish hair. Sensitivity is his middle name, and his clothes fit badly at certain points. On seeing the women at the window, he is worried that something has happened.*)

AAZAM. Y'Allah!! (*He rushes to the window.*)

MARIA (*turning to him*). Sssssst! (AAZAM *sees the baby is all right, and they all start back downstage.*)

FAREEDEH. Don't bother to hush him. She won't wake up until she gets hungry. (*She sits at the mortar and starts pounding.*)

AAZAM. Thank Allah, everything's all right. (*He is at the edge of the center step, right of center, shaking hands with* MARIA.) How are you, Maria? How's your sister? How's her husband? How're her children?

MARIA. Very well. Very well, thank you.

AAZAM. You got back just today?

MARIA. Today.

AAZAM. And the journey was easy?

MARIA. It was all right. Selim brought me on his donkey.

AAZAM. Yeeee! Selim has come? Where's he staying?

MARIA. At Sheikh Mohammed's.

AAZAM. I must go see him. (*He steps down and starts for the door at left.* MARIA *resumes her former seat.* AAZAM *stops.*) Fareedeh, you're watching Hesta well?

FAREEDEH. Y'Allah, I'm watching her as well as I can. It's not so easy to fix food and run to the window all the time. (*She stops pounding and turns toward* AAZAM.) In fact, my dear brother-in-law, I think it's high time something were done about Hesta.

AAZAM. What d'you mean, "done about Hesta"?

FAREEDEH. I mean what I say.

MARIA. You mean, give the baby to someone else to nurse?

FAREEDEH. No, no, no. That wouldn't help Hesta, at all. She wouldn't know the difference, without the baby to wake her up. (*Pounding.*) Y'Allah, no. What she needs is something to make her more lively, something to—well—to give her more ... umph.

AAZAM. Eh—yes. I must say, I've thought that would be a good thing, more than once. You know, it's rather awkward for me in the village. Everyone talks about it, especially now with the new boy. But what can a husband do? After all, I'm not a doctor, I've never taken ...

FAREEDEH. Who said anything about your being a doctor? Nobody said it was your fault.

AAZAM. Nooooo. But after all a man is responsible for his wife, in a way, and ...(*Listens.*)

MARIA. What's the matter? (FAREEDEH *stops pounding.*)

AAZAM. Listen. The baby doesn't cry very much, does he?

FAREEDEH. No, thank Allah.

AAZAM. Shouldn't he cry a little now and then?

FAREEDEH. And why now? He's just nursed so there's no reason for him to cry.

AAZAM (*easing towards window*). All the same, it seems to me, if I were a baby, and could do nothing but eat, sleep, and cry, I'd spend... Y'Allah! (*He is at the window.*) She's on the baby! (*The others rush up to the window shouting.*)

FAREEDEH *and* MARIA (*as they run*). Hesta! Hesta! (*At the window.*) Hesta! Wake up! You're on the baby!

HESTA'S VOICE. Ayayayayee!! [1] My son, my baby, my sweet little boy!
(*Baby's cries are heard. Group at window relax. Baby's cries continue audibly and fade throughout the following, as* HESTA *tries to quiet it.*)

ALL (*ad libbing*). 'Smallah! He's all right! Ayayayayay! May Allah be praised! etc.
(*All back away from the window,* AAZAM *leaning against the wall at left,* FAREEDEH *against wall up center, and* MARIA *against house wall downstage of the window.*)

AAZAM. Allah! That was a close shave. And you, Fareedeh, why weren't you watching them?

FAREEDEH. And why wasn't I watching them? Yeeee! And why weren't you watching them? (*Stepping towards* AAZAM.) Were you making kibbeh? No. Were you picking through the lentils? No.

1. Pronounced "ah-i-ah-i-ah-i-ah-ee!!" (rapidly).

AAZAM. But I might not have been here. I might have been in the shop. No one would have gone up to that window. The baby . . .

FAREEDEH. So no one would have gone to the window. (*She starts back to bench.*) So now let's not fight with each other.
(MARIA *also sits where she was.* FAREEDEH *starts pounding.*)

MARIA. Fareedeh. What you said before—something must be done about Hesta.

FAREEDEH. You're telling me? I'm telling Aazam!

AAZAM. But I *know* something must be done. (*Coming downstage.*) But what can I do?

MARIA. You might ask Selim. He's a very wise man. While he brought me here on his donkey, he told me about the time he wrote a letter for a friend to get the friend a bride from his cousins up north. (FA-REEDEH *stops pounding and listens.*) The letter was so nice that the girl's family accepted him at once without even seeing him.

FAREEDEH. Yeeee! He's a wise and clever man. Go find him, Aazam, and bring him here. We must do something quickly, quickly, quickly before Hesta again falls asleep. (MARIA *and* AAZAM *turn towards window at this remark.*)

AAZAM. You say Selim is at Sheikh Mohammed's?

MARIA. Yes, if he's still there.

AAZAM. I'll go see if I can find him. Maybe he can think of some way. (*On his way to the door at left.*) Maybe he has some kind of medicine from the city that will help. (*Off.*) Good-bye.

FAREEDEH *and* MARIA. Good-bye!

FAREEDEH. Come back quickly! (FAREEDEH *resumes her pounding and* MARIA *takes up the platter of lentils and picks* [1] *over them.*) Ach, I hope Selim can think of something. (*Pause.*) D'you know why he came here?

MARIA. Oh, you know, he goes to bring things from the city and this time was coming through Ainab again; and so he brought me back. (*Laughs.*) You know, Najla said everyone in the village is trying to get him to marry again and settle down.

FAREEDEH. And why doesn't he?

MARIA. Well, I guess he hasn't found the right wife.

HESTA'S VOICE. Where's Aazam gone?

FAREEDEH. Aazam? He went to the shop.

HESTA'S VOICE. What was he doing here at this hour?

MARIA (*running up to the window*). Hesta! Hello! How are you! How's the baby?

HESTA'S VOICE. Maria! My sweet! Yeeee! You look so pretty! I'm well. And you? How did you find Najla, and her husband and the children? Are they well?

---

1. This involves picking out any little stones or other extraneous matter found among the lentils.

MARIA. Yes, thank you. They're all quite well now. And you had your baby while I was away! (*Leaning in window.*) 'Ismallah! Isn't he a sweet one. May Allah be with him and protect him all his life.

HESTA'S VOICE (*laughing*). Thank you, thank you. Ach, my little dear, sweet one. My baby! My little boy! Look, Maria, his hair is like Sheikh Mohammed's—a little here—a little there. (*Both laugh.*)

MARIA. Ahh. But his cheeks are like two ripe pomegranates. Like yours.

FAREEDEH (*as she works*). Hesta's cheeks aren't like pomegranates. They're more like over-ripe plums!

HESTA. Yeee! (*Laughing, she sits up and her head and shoulders appear above window sill.*) How delicious I must look! Ya, Fareedeh? Have we any figs on our trees yet?

FAREEDEH. And when would I've had a chance to look? I haven't been out on the hill here for more than a week now, with you and the baby, and the food to fix and the house to clean.

HESTA. Ach, you're so busy. Why don't you stop working sometimes and rest a little? Why d'you have to make kibbeh today?

FAREEDEH. Tomorrow's the seventh day, and everybody'll be expecting it. (*She stops and turns towards window.*) It's not often we've celebrated the seventh day after the baby comes, heh?

HESTA. Ach, no! (*Looking down at baby beside her.*) Ayayayayay, and to think... just now ... ayayay ... my little pomegranate, my sweet, sweet, sweet little pomegranate! Fareedeh, when will you go out to see if there are any figs? I feel I could eat some very easily, you know. (*Sounds of* AAZAM *and* SELIM'S *voices approaching are heard.* MARIA *and* FAREEDEH *look at each other.*)

MARIA. Go to sleep now, Hesta, and I'll go out on the hill here in a little while and look, and if there are any ripe ones, I'll bring them to you—as many as the basket will hold.

HESTA. Ach, Maria, that'll be very nice. Yeee, you are a dear. (*Yawning.*) Ahhhch. (*She settles back on her mat with satisfied grunts.* AAZAM *and* SELIM'S *voices have grown louder as they approach, and now they enter, talking excitedly.* SELIM *is in his late thirties, a product of the mountains with a dash of the city about him. He is portly, but not pompous, and he accepts the recognition of his superior intellect with attempted humility.*)

FAREEDEH (*rushing to quiet them as she opens door at left*). Sssst! She's still awake, and if she hears you, she'll want to know what's going on. (*They nod understandingly as they enter.* AAZAM *crosses to door of house at right, goes in to bring out chairs.* FAREEDEH *and* SELIM *are at the door, left.*) And you, Selim, how are you? It's a long time since we've seen you here. How's your father, how're your sisters, how're your brothers? All well?

SELIM. Yes, thank you, thank you, and you? Are you well?

FAREEDEH. As well as can be. Yaani ... (*She looks down smiling—embarrassed.*)

MARIA. Hello, Selim. (*She meets him at center and shakes hands.*)

SELIM. Hello, Maria.

AAZAM (*coming out of house with two chairs and placing them at center stage*). Let's get down to business. Come, Selim, sit down here. (MARIA *and* FAREEDEH *go to their places but do not work.*)

SELIM. Thank you. (*He sits in center chair.* AAZAM *sits in the one left of center.*)

AAZAM. I've just been telling him, Fareedeh, on the way over, about Hesta.

FAREEDEH. Ya, Selim. It's really bad the way she's so lazy. She sleeps all night and almost all morning, and in the afternoon most of the time; and the rest of the time she just sews and eats and now, of course, she has to nurse the baby.

SELIM. That's not so good, is it? You have to do all the work, then?

FAREEDEH. Do all the work!? The only thing I don't have to do is to sleep for Hesta!

AAZAM. Yeee. I'm sure I don't know what I'd do without Fareedeh. But you know, Hesta means well. She's really very kind. It's just that—well—that Allah has made her a little lazy, you know.

SELIM (*playing with his beads* [1]). Yes, yes.

FAREEDEH. What d'you think we should do? (*Pause as everyone is thinking.*) After all there must be some way of making her more lively. It can't be the way Allah intended her to be. Would he take all that trouble to bring her those babies and then make her so that she sleeps on them all? No, if you ask me.

SELIM. You're right. It isn't natural. We should find something to do that will make her more lively.

MARIA. Why not prick her with pins?

AAZAM. Prick her with pins? Yeee, that would hurt her too much. Besides, you can't go around pricking her with pins all day to make her busy. Who'd do that? I certainly wouldn't.

FAREEDEH. I would!

SELIM. No, that won't do, because still no one could leave her alone with the baby. No, we must do something to her that will stay with her, something that will make her lively of its own self.

FAREEDEH. That's good. Yes... (*All think.*) Maybe something for her to eat. In that way it would stay inside her, no?

SELIM. Ye-e-es. Yes! What kind of food is there that makes one feel very lively?

1. A string of large amber beads, strung loosely on a string about twelve inches in diameter, with a short tassle hanging from it. The men carry these in their pockets, pulling them out to finger, in the manner in which we use our watch chains.

MARIA. Something that burns.

AAZAM. Ach, but that would hurt her!

MARIA. Not badly.

AAZAM. But there'd be no point in that, because once she stopped jumping about on account of the burning, she'd feel bad, and that would make her lazy—even more lazy again.

SELIM. You know what I think. I think that it must be something that's lively itself, which by being eaten, would naturally make her so.

FAREEDEH. Yeeee! You mean like a young donkey?

MARIA. How could she eat a young donkey?

FAREEDEH. Foolish! She couldn't eat a young donkey, of course, but she could eat a part of one.

SELIM. No, no, no. Don't you see, that wouldn't do at all! The thing must be altogether alive and very active.

AAZAM. A grasshopper! A grasshopper is smaller, and it certainly is lively.

MARIA. But she couldn't swallow a grasshopper whole. She'd have to chew it, and then that wouldn't do any good.

FAREEDEH. Besides, Hesta's no dumb one. You couldn't fool her with a live grasshopper.

AAZAM. Yes. That's true. (*Pause as all think.*)

SELIM. I know what! Fleas!

ALL. Fleas?

SELIM. Why not, fleas? They're the most active things, and besides they're so small she wouldn't know she was eating them.

FAREEDEH. Ayayayayay! And how do you propose to keep the fleas in one place long enough to get them in her mouth?

SELIM. Well, what does she like to eat especially?

AAZAM. Yeeeee, but that's a good idea! What does she like to eat especially, Fareedeh?

FAREEDEH. She likes kibbeh.

AAZAM. That's an idea. And Fareedeh's just preparing some kibbeh, and could slip a few in.

SELIM. But then they'd be cooked! Don't you see, they must still be lively in order to make her lively!

HESTA'S VOICE. Who's there? (*All stop, realizing they've raised their voices too high.* AAZAM *is about to answer, when* FAREEDEH *jumps up and claps her hand over his mouth.*)

FAREEDEH. Oh, Hesta, it's only a man selling needles and thread.

HESTA'S VOICE. Buy some, buy some, and tell him to stop shouting.

FAREEDEH. All right. (*Pause as* FAREEDEH *goes back to bench.*)

HESTA'S VOICE. What colors did you get?

FAREEDEH. Eh-h-h ... white and black.

HESTA'S VOICE. Ohhh. Why didn't you get some red for the flower in the corner?

FAREEDEH. Eh-h-h ... next time, next time I'll get some.

HESTA'S VOICE. Run after him and get some. Ple-e-ease!

FAREEDEH. But how can I run after him and get some, when I have the kibbeh to do? (*She starts pounding determinedly.*) Why don't you go?

HESTA'S VOICE. I go? Sabrunjameen! [1] (*She groans, grunts, and then is silent.*)

FAREEDEH (*stops pounding*). You see. (SELIM *nods.*) So, now, what's your suggestion? How will we give her the fleas so they're not cooked and so they don't jump away, and also so that she doesn't know she's eating them?

SELIM. Well, what else does she like? What kind of fruit?

MARIA. Oh, she likes figs. She just asked me, before you came, to go and bring her some from the trees, if they're ripe.

1. An ejaculation.

SELIM. Figs? Ach, that'd be wonderful. We could just open the figs a little—just enough to put the fleas in, close them, so the fleas don't jump out, and she wouldn't know the difference.

AAZAM. Brilliant! Brilliant! They'll seem just like the inside of the fig!

FAREEDEH. Yeee! Selim! So you think that will really do it?

SELIM. And why not? Could anything be more logical?

FAREEDEH. No...No... (*Picking up basket at corner of house.*) Quickly, Maria, take this basket and run and bring some figs. Never mind if they're not quite ripe. Bring what you can and quick, before she wakes up again.
(MARIA *takes the basket from* FAREEDEH *and hurries off through the gate upstage.* FAREEDEH *goes back to the bench and pounds.*)

AAZAM. Really, Selim, that's the best thought! You're a very clever man. If I had your cleverness, I wouldn't stay around here in the mountains. I'd go down to the city and set up a shop. Why don't you start business down there?

SELIM. Me! (*Glancing at* FAREEDEH.) Well, after all, at first I must find another wife. I must do that before I can set up house again away from my family.

AAZAM. Poor Julia, may Allah be with her, she was a good wife to you, eh, Selim?—Though she didn't bear you any children.

SELIM. She was a good wife. (*Looking at* FAREEDEH.) There are others that should make good wives, too.

AAZAM (*noticing his glance*). Yeeeee! Of course! And why not. (*Laughs and slaps his knee.* SELIM *laughs too.* FAREEDEH *looks up to find what they're laughing at, and sees them looking at her. She catches their meaning, becomes fussed, giggles.*) And why not, eh, Fareedeh? (*She doesn't answer, but giggles.*) Fareedeh'd make you a good wife. She cooks well. And what do you say, Fareedeh?

FAREEDEH (*pause*). And where would you all be, I'd like to know, if I went off, huh?

AAZAM. Yeee! I didn't think of that.

SELIM. You don't have to worry about that now, if the fleas work.

AAZAM. Yes, of course... of course. We *must* arrange it. Ayayayayay...

MARIA (*coming back with the figs, and going to* FAREEDEH). Here. Here are the figs that were the ripest. (FAREEDEH *takes them and hands a couple to each person*).

FAREEDEH. Here. Each one take two and fill them.

AAZAM. Good. And now where will we find the most fleas?

FAREEDEH. Over there by the wall in the shade where the dog usually lies. (*Points to projecting buttress at stage left.*)

AAZAM. Good. (*He dashes over there. The others follow. As they look, fleas collect on their legs and skirts at the bottom. As they catch them, they put them in their figs.*)

SELIM (*pinning one on his leg*). I've got one!

MARIA (*chasing one along the ground*). Oh, I just missed it!

AAZAM (*spotting one on* SELIM's *leg*). Hold still! Hold still, Selim! I see one on your leg. (*He aims and pins it. They continue to stalk fleas in that area, exclaiming as they stalk. The chair, stage left, is suddenly knocked over, which wakes* HESTA.)

HESTA'S VOICE. What fell? (*All hold their various positions, whatever they may be, as though petrified.*)

FAREEDEH. Oh, I just knocked over the bench.

HESTA'S VOICE. Is Maria there?

MARIA. Yes?

HESTA'S VOICE. Have you brought those figs yet?

MARIA. Yes, I just brought them. (*She collects them quickly from the others and goes up to the window. The others stand stage left watching breathlessly.*)

HESTA'S VOICE. Ach, good. I could eat four at one gulp.

MARIA. Good. Here they are.

HESTA (*appearing at the window, sitting on the floor*). Give them here. (*She pokes one in her mouth, and sees the other people.*) Yeeee! What are you two doing here? Selim! How are you? (*He goes up and shakes hands.* MARIA *is upstage of the window.*) How's your father? How's your mother?

SELIM. Very well, thank you.

HESTA. Have a fig? (*Pause as* SELIM *looks around desperately for an un-fleaed fig.*)

SELIM. Uh—thank you, no. I've just been eating.

HESTA. But these—these are the first figs from our trees this year. They're fresh off the trees. Maria just brought them to me.

SELIM. Thank you. Thank you. (*He starts backing to the wall stage left, very slowly.*) I really am not hungry. (HESTA *reaches out across the window sill and pulls him down and puts one in his mouth.*)

HESTA. Don't be polite. Take it. (HESTA *eats one, and with her mouth full, continues.*) And you, Maria, you must share our first figs too. Here.

MARIA. No, really. I couldn't.

HESTA. But why not? Are you ill? A fig is not so large that it takes much eating! Mmmmm, they're so good. Really, you know, I don't think I've ever tasted better. (*She gets up, so she is standing in the window, leans over the sill, and heaves herself slowly over it. As she stands up triumphant, outside the window, she notices the others.*) What's the matter? Heh? (SELIM *is at the upstage corner of the house,* MARIA *at center, and* AAZAM *and* FAREEDEH *down stage left, all staring wide-eyed and open-mouthed at* HESTA.)

FAREEDEH. Ehhhh ... nothing.

HESTA. Then why do you all stand like dummies and not eat any figs?

FAREEDEH. Well—ehh ... there are only a few, and since you asked especially for them, you should have them.

HESTA. Nonsense! This isn't my house for me to sit and eat while everyone else goes hungry. (*She picks up the figs off the sill, goes to* MARIA *and forces a fig in her mouth, her movements getting more and more energetic.*) Here, you must eat one.

FAREEDEH (*realizing her turn is next*). Yeeee, I forgot, I must go pick the radishes for this noon! (*She makes for the garden gate upstage, but* HESTA *meets her left of center and forces her to take a fig.*)

HESTA. Why must you get the radishes? I'll get the radishes ... later. Now we must enjoy our first figs of the season. You work too hard! (AAZAM *has meanwhile hidden behind the angle of the wall left.*) And where is Aazam? (*She runs down towards the front door.*)

SELIM (*swallowing the last of his fig*). He must have gone out a moment. (MARIA *giggles,* FAREEDEH *follows,* SELIM *is drawn in.* HESTA, *seeing them, catches the spark. They all laugh.*)

HESTA. I don't know what you're laughing at, but it's very funny.

AAZAM (*with an awed exclamation*). Y'Allah! (*He comes out from behind the buttress cautiously and goes to center to shake* SELIM's *hand.*) Congratulations, my dear Selim!

HESTA. Yeeee! Where were you? Why must you congratulate Selim? (AAZAM *is about to answer when* FAREEDEH *raps him one on his front and pushes him upstage.*)

SELIM. Well, you see, Hesta, I've asked for Fareedeh for my wife and—well—I've won her.

HESTA. Ayayay! (*She runs to* FAREEDEH *and kisses her on both cheeks, calling her all kinds of endearing names.* MARIA *dashes over and joins in while* AAZAM *and* SELIM *exchange handshakes, pats on backs, and knowing looks,* AAZAM *getting the better of it.* HESTA, *breaking into song, starts dancing in the middle of the stage and the others join in, clapping their hands in accompaniment, except* AAZAM, *who stands at stage right overcome and awed at the goings on. Suddenly the baby's cries are heard, the singing stops, and all stand for a moment frozen, then dash for the window.*)

CURTAIN

CHINA
THE WANDERING DRAGON

BY *T'ang Wen Shun*

THE CHARACTERS

As originally produced by The Carolina Playmakers on their Eightieth Bill of Experimental Productions of New Plays in the Playmakers Theatre, Chapel Hill, North Carolina, February 13, 1942. First published in THE CAROLINA PLAY-BOOK *for March, 1942.*

THE PROPERTY MAN .... Russell Rogers
THE GOD OF EARTH .... Arthur Conescu
THE GODDESS OF EARTH .... Buddie Westover
LEE LUNG, *keeper of the Inn* .... William Rawls
LEE MU, *his mother, a widow* ...... Josephine Sharkey
LEE FONG FONG, *her daughter* .... Jean McKenzie
LEE SHIAO FONG,
    younger sister of Fong Fong ...... Louise Stumberg
THE CARRIAGE MAN .... Wynn Williams
THE EMPEROR, CHENG TE .... Robert Schenkkan
THE EMPEROR'S ATTENDANT .... Frank Groseclose
TWO GUARDS .... Wynn Williams, Hampton Hubbard

THE SCENE: The Inn of Lee Lung, in the Town of Mai Lung, Chiangsi Province, South China.

THE TIME: The Ming Dynasty, the sixteenth century. A morning in November.

THE SCENE

The action of the play takes place in the Town of Mai Lung in three different localities: an open field, the gateway of the Inn of Lee Lung, and the reception hall inside the Inn. The setting is simply a richly-embroidered tapestry or decorated screen, with two entrances at the rear. The one at the right leads outside; the one at the left leads to the inner rooms of the Inn.

A table upstage, center, with a chair on each side, constitutes all the furniture needed. The table and the chairs should be covered with embroidered cloths and the chairs should have cushions. A chair at the extreme right, downstage, serves as the hitching post of the Inn.

The Property Man sits on a chair downstage, left. Since he has a great many properties, he may place some of them on a table in front of him and leave the others backstage, going out for them as they are needed. The attitude of The Property Man is altogether casual; nothing disturbs him and his bland expression never changes. He goes about his business as a matter of course; neither the actors nor the audience pay any attention to him. On the Chinese stage he is invisible!

It is a common practice in the Chinese theatre for a man to play the part of an old woman. In this play The Goddess of Earth should be played by a man costumed as a woman and speaking in a falsetto voice. The mother, Lee Mu, however, should be played by an elderly woman. The entrance of each character is accompanied by a musical instrument, a drum for The God and

GODDESS OF EARTH, *a wooden block for* LEE MU, *a bell for* LEE LUNG, *a soft cymbal for the heroine,* FONG FONG. *Whenever a character makes an entrance his particular instrument is sounded. This helps to establish the character clearly.*

Precise body movements, especially of the hands, are essential to Chinese acting. The walk of the heroine should have grace and ease and a buoyant quality. She should never walk in a straight line, especially when she is making an exit. The straight line would make her seem aggressive, too direct. Rather, she should move in a lady-like curve. Since few facial expressions are used by the Chinese actor, the hands are called upon to express sentiments ordinarily conveyed by the face. Symbolic gestures are employed to express certain meanings and emotions. For instance, whenever the word "Buddha" is mentioned, the character speaking the word will fold his hands above his head to indicate respect. Whenever a character mentions himself, he indicates himself with a gesture of the hand.

Three strokes of a gong are heard as the curtains open. THE PROPERTY MAN *is seen contentedly smoking his pipe. His eyes are closed. Evidently he is weary. But casually he takes up a drum and beats on it rhythmically.*

At the sound THE GOD *and* GODDESS OF EARTH *appear, one from each side,* THE GOD *from the left and* THE GODDESS *from the right.* THE GOD OF EARTH *wears a yellow robe and appears to be more than eighty years old.* THE GODDESS OF EARTH, *who can be any age from forty to seventy, wears a blue richly-embroidered robe. Each of them carries a cane in the right hand and has a horsehair whip in the left. A whip of this kind does not mean horseback riding; it signifies deity and invisibility. As* THE GOD *and* GODDESS OF EARTH *meet at the center of the stage, they bow to each other deeply. Then they turn and face the audience.*

THE GOD and GODDESS OF EARTH. I am God of Earth. I am Goddess of Earth.

THE GOD OF EARTH. Know you, Lao Par, old companion, what day is today?

THE GODDESS OF EARTH. The fifteenth day of the eleventh month of the thirteenth year of the reign of the Emperor, Cheng Te, of Ta Ming.

THE GOD OF EARTH. Know you the significance of to-day?

THE GODDESS OF EARTH (*slowly shaking her head*). No significance.

THE GOD OF EARTH. An imperial order from the Buddha, the Supreme Lord of all gods in the thirteenth Heaven has come to me notifying me that the Emperor Cheng Te of Ta Ming will make his primary august appearance in this most humble town of Mai Lung. We, being the God and Goddess of Earth, are officially appointed as the guiding host and hostess to His Majesty, Cheng Te, Lord of Ten Thousand Years.

THE GODDESS OF EARTH (*looking around*). Is His Majesty approaching soon?

THE GOD OF EARTH. My eyesight is dim. Let us climb the mountain of Tai-Shan. Perhaps we may discern and perceive His Majesty's celestial, golden flame blazing toward the ethereal firmament.
(*They go toward the table upstage, center. They try*

to get up on the chair first, but fail to do so. THE GOD
OF EARTH *helps* THE GODDESS *to get up; then finds himself incapable of mounting higher.* THE GODDESS *gets
down from the chair and helps* THE GOD *up on it.
Finding herself still at the foot of the mountain, she
waves her horsehair whip for help. The awkward
silence wakes up* THE PROPERTY MAN *and he comes to
their rescue. Using the chair on each side of the table
as a stepping stone, both of them mount the table.
Standing and shading their eyes with their hands, they
stretch forward to discover the objects imagined
thousands of feet below.*)

THE GODDESS OF EARTH (*looking off*). Do you see anything?

THE GOD OF EARTH. See, Lao Par, His Majesty is approaching the boundary line of the town of Mai Lung.
(*They bow deeply.*) We, as God and Goddess of
Earth, welcome Your Majesty, Son of Heaven, with
unlaced boots and exposed elbows.[1] (*They bow
deeply.*) Hurry, we must, to the Lee Lung Inn which
His Majesty will make his royal residence for the time
being. (*They step down from the table by the chairs
with the help of* THE PROPERTY MAN. *They bow to
each other and leave by the two doors at the rear,* THE
GOD OF EARTH *going left,* THE GODDESS, *right.*)
(THE PROPERTY MAN *takes up a wooden signboard
inscribed "LEE LUNG INN, TOWN OF MAI
LUNG" and places it on the back of a chair downstage, right. The chair is used not only as a support
for the sign, but also as a hitching post where the horses
of various characters are tied.*)

1. Marks of respect.

(*The scene has now changed from the open field to
the waiting room of the Inn.*)

(The Property Man *goes back to his place and rings
a bell. At the sound of the bell* Lee Lung *comes running in, right. In his right hand he holds a whip indicating that he is riding. His whip is made of silk cords,
different from those of* The God *and* Goddess of
Earth.)

(Lee Lung *is a man of twenty-two, dull and simple.
He pantomimes getting off his donkey and fastening
it to the hitching post; then he throws down the whip.*)

Lee Lung (*to the donkey*). Halt, wait for me here, old
friend. I shall go to inform my Reverend Mother, your
old mistress, of my impending journey. (*He lifts his
feet over the imaginary threshold, enters the house,
and bows deeply.*) My most Reverend Mother, your
son, Lung, wishes to speak to you. (*He bows again.*)
(The Property Man *beats on a wooden block, and
at the sound* Lee Mu, *the Mother, appears from the
left. She is an elderly woman of about fifty years, dignified, full of vigor and quick tempered, but always
graceful. She wears a black robe with silver embroidery.* The Property Man *places a chair before the
table for her and she sits.*)

Lee Mu. What is your wish, my son?

Lee Lung (*hesitating*). You mentioned . . . that is . . . you
planned . . . Mother, permit me to remind you that today we are to pay a visit to the honorable family of
Chao in the neighboring town of Yang Lin.

Lee Mu. The family of Chao?

LEE LUNG. I believe that you have some settlement to discuss with the eminent elder father, Chao—I mean, some affair which may concern their elegant daughter and perhaps, probably, or possibly, myself?

LEE MU. Ay, perhaps . . . possibly . . . probably. Fetch me the Book of Dates and Dreams. I desire to find out if today is the day of the yellow-road. I refuse to go on a journey if it is the day of the black-road.

LEE LUNG. Today is the day of the yellow-road. I studied the Book of Dates and Dreams this morning. Besides, the God of Prosperity is facing north this morning at the eleventh hour. We will meet his golden chariot if we start at once. The Book cannot be wrong.

LEE MU. That makes me remember something. Your sister, Fong Fong, has asked for the Book of Dates and Dreams. She had a dream last night. Tell her to bring in my morning tea and she can look for the meaning of her dream here.

LEE LUNG. Yes, Mother. But are we going to Yang Lin to visit the family of Chao? There is only one yellow day in a month.

LEE MU. You seem anxious, my son. It is your mother who is to see the maid, therefore why be so impatient?

LEE LUNG. But . . . but . . . my most understanding mother, what is to become of me?

LEE MU. Wait till the six ceremonies are over. We will need you then at the last ceremony when the bride is brought here; that is, if I can obtain a bride for you.

But not until then. I hope that I have made it clear enough for my son to understand.

LEE LUNG. Yes, but do you need me today, my patient mother?

LEE MU. No—yes! See that my carriage is ready.

LEE LUNG. So you will go?

LEE MU. Not until I finish my morning tea. Where is your donkey?

LEE LUNG. He is waiting outside the Inn. Ah-ya, I forgot to call Fong Fong. (*He calls.*) Fong Fong, Mother's morning tea.
(THE PROPERTY MAN *strikes a tiny cymbal, softly. At the sound of the cymbal* FONG FONG *appears from the left. She is about eighteen years old, blooming and charming. She is gentle and obedient. She wears a light pink silk embroidered robe.*)
(*She extends her left hand toward* THE PROPERTY MAN, *who hands her a cup on a tray. Without looking at* THE PROPERTY MAN *she takes the tray and walks toward her mother.*)

FONG FONG. Your daughter wishes you morning peace, Reverend Mother. (*She bows and hands* LEE MU *the cup of tea.*) Your morning tea.

LEE MU (*receives the cup. Shading her face with one hand, she drinks the tea*). Lung, fetch me the Book of Dates and Dreams. (THE PROPERTY MAN *hands him the book and he gives it to* LEE MU.) Fong Fong, what did you dream of last night?

FONG FONG. I dreamed of a fiery dragon tightly coiling around my body. It almost suffocated me to death, my bed-chamber seemed to be all blazing with flames. I was greatly frightened. I cried, but no one came to my rescue. I thought I was doomed to die.

LEE MU. Fire and flames? (*She is looking at the book.*) There are ten lines of characters about fire and flames in the book. What do they mean? (*She hands the book to* LEE LUNG, *who looks at it, shakes his head, and hands it back to her.*) It is obvious enough, is it not? Heaven is going to pour down fire and flames on our house. (*Becoming alarmed.*) Fong Fong, why did you dream of fire and flames? Did you not know that there are ten thousand other things to dream about? And the dragon, what does that signify? (*She looks at the book again, although she knows perfectly well that she will not be able to make out anything from it.*) There is no mention about dragons here. Fong Fong, are you certain that the dragon is not a turtle or a serpent?

FONG FONG. I am not certain, but I know it was not a turtle. It had claws and horns.

LEE MU. I know the turtle signifies long life and the dragon, famine and starvation. Fong Fong, you stupid, wooden-headed girl, how could you have dreamed that? You have brought destruction on the family. What have we done to deserve this? (*Rising and lifting her eyes to heaven.*) My merciful heaven, spare my family! For seven generations we have lived in peace and contentment, we have never failed to say our morning prayers, or ever forgotten to celebrate your birthday. I always roast a pig for you on the first day of the year. If Fong Fong has in any way offended you, punish her, but spare the rest of my family. I have but one son to continue the ancestral line.

LEE LUNG (*appealing to heaven*). I am not responsible for Fong Fong's misconduct. Please do not include me in your wrath. You cannot punish me. I—I am about to be married! (*To* FONG FONG.) See what you have done? You have completely upset our Reverend Mother, and me, your honorable brother. Dreaming of fire and the dragon, how foolish!

FONG FONG. Heaven forbid that misfortune should ever befall this house.

LEE MU. We will have to appease the wrath of our Buddha before we leave. Lung, go and fetch the candles, the incense, the tripod, and seventy pieces of yellow-money. Fong Fong, kneel down and face the East. (THE PROPERTY MAN *hands* LEE LUNG *two candles, the incense, tripod, and some pieces of yellow-money on a tray.* LEE LUNG *lights the candles and the incense.* LEE MU *holds the tripod above* FONG FONG's *head and prays with eyes closed.*) Ah me tao foo! Ah me tao foo! [1]

LEE LUNG (*impatient*). Mother, the morning has almost approached the eleventh hour.

LEE MU (*ignoring him*). Ah me tao foo!

FONG FONG (*folding her hands, she closes her eyes, and prays.* THE PROPERTY MAN *throws a cushion for her to kneel on*). Ah me tao foo! Punish me, righteous

1. Buddha.

Buddha, if I have offended you. But do not bring fire and starvation to my mother, my brother, and my sister. If I have offended you, I deserve to die. (*She weeps.*)

(THE PROPERTY MAN *strikes another tiny gong and* SHIAO FONG *appears. She is the second daughter of* LEE MU, *bright and cheerful and full of spirit. She wears a light green embroidered robe.*)

SHIAO FONG. Mother, you have just finished your morning prayer to our Buddha. What ceremony is this?

LEE MU. Little girls are not to question what their elders are doing. Face the East and kowtow [1] to our Buddha. (SHIAO FONG *and* FONG FONG *do so.* THE PROPERTY MAN *throws another cushion for* SHIAO FONG *to kneel on.*) Ask Buddha to bless our trip to Yang Lin.

SHIAO FONG. Is this another one of my respected brother's betrothal ventures, Mother?

LEE MU. A maiden ought to know when to refrain from inquiries, especially from those that concern matrimony.

SHIAO FONG. But a sister-in-law sounds so strange, Mother. I would rather have a brother-in-law first.

FONG FONG. You do not know what you are saying, my sister.

SHIAO FONG. Ay-ya, I forgot that it would concern you too—naturally. (*Looking at* FONG FONG *with eyes full of mischief.*)

1. To kneel and bow the head.

LEE LUNG (*impatient*). My most patient mother, we will miss the God of Prosperity if we retard our journey thus. My donkey must be exhausted with standing so long.

LEE MU (*to both maidens*). I want you both to look after the Inn while we are away. Probably there will not be any customers at this time of the day. If there should be, tell them to wait till we come back. Where is my carriage?

LEE LUNG. It is outside with the donkey.
(*They all leave the Inn, each crossing the threshold in pantomime, lifting his feet.* THE CARRIAGE MAN *comes in from the right entrance, holding in each hand a bamboo pole with a square of white cloth attached, with a wheel painted on each. These constitute the carriage.* LEE MU *stands between the two wheels indicating that she is in the carriage.* LEE LUNG *unfastens the donkey, picks up the whip, and mounts in pantomime. The girls bow reverently.*)

LEE LUNG (*to* FONG FONG). If we fail in this attempt, I have no one to blame but you. (*With a quick wave of his whip, he follows* LEE MU *out right.* THE PROPERTY MAN *rings the bell.*)

FONG FONG. How I dread the hour of their reappearance. Buddha, be merciful! (*She goes into the Inn, stepping over the threshold.* SHIAO FONG *follows her.*) Here I must wait patiently for the unfolding of my fate. (*She looks around the reception hall.*) Shall we clean the hall while we are waiting for the safe return of our mother and our brother?

SHIAO FONG (*sitting*). I am tired today. You clean the hall while I rest.

FONG FONG. Then you wash the horse-post outside.
(*With a sigh* SHIAO FONG, *rising, extends her hand to* THE PROPERTY MAN *without looking at him. He hands her a towel and she goes outside right, to the chair which serves as the horse-post, and begins washing it in pantomime.*)
(*In the meantime* THE PROPERTY MAN *furnishes* FONG FONG *with an empty basin and a dry towel.* FONG FONG *removes the candles and the tripod; then begins washing the table and chairs in pantomime. When she finishes the cleaning, she empties the basin toward the audience. Chinese music is played during the pantomime.*)
(*Now* THE EMPEROR, CHENG TE, *comes in from the right, holding a whip in his hand to indicate that he is on horseback. He is about forty years old and is dressed in a deep purple gown, with a travelling cloak and hat.* THE GOD *and* GODDESS OF EARTH *walk protectingly beside him. He halts at the horse-post.* SHIAO FONG *sees him coming.*)

SHIAO FONG. Fong Fong, a man! (*She runs in dragging* FONG FONG *behind her.* FONG FONG *hurriedly throws the towel and basin to* THE PROPERTY MAN *and runs within, upstage left.*)
(CHENG TE *dismounts and pantomimes fastening his horse to the hitching post, throwing down his whip.* THE GOD *and* GODDESS OF EARTH *help him down and bow deeply to him before they leave by the right entrance.* CHENG TE *examines the inscription on the Inn.*)

CHENG TE. "Lee Lung Inn, Town of Mai Lung!" At last we have found a place for lodging.

(CHENG TE *walks into the Inn and takes the chair which* THE PROPERTY MAN *has placed for him behind the table. He rubs his eyes to indicate that he is weary. He waits a moment. Nothing happens. He pounds on the table for service. No response. He does so again. Still no answer. Becoming impatient, he pounds loudly three times in rapid succession.* THE GOD *and* GODDESS OF EARTH *enter from the right, evidently alarmed. They come in while* CHENG TE *is striking the table for the fourth time. They look and nod to each other understandingly. With their whips they point to the left entrance, go within, and lead* FONG FONG *out.* FONG FONG *stands silent with her back toward* THE EMPEROR. THE GODS *glance from her to* THE EMPEROR, *who is beating on the table for the fifth time. They look helpless, but having done their duty they leave by the left entrance.* FONG FONG *stands silent, and there is an awkward pause while* CHENG TE *pounds the table for the last time.*)

FONG FONG. Your humble maid is at your service, Venerable Sir.

CHENG TE. We are suffering from extreme thirst and exhaustion. My poor steed is almost on the verge of collapse. We request immediate service. Attend my horse at once.

FONG FONG. Aye, Venerable Sir. (*She goes outside, takes up the whip to unfasten the horse, and delivers it in pantomime to* THE PROPERTY MAN. FONG FONG *returns to the reception room of the Inn.*) Any other orders, Venerable Sir? (*For the first time they look into each other's faces. Each is struck by the unusually attractive appearance of the other.*)

CHENG TE. My fair almond-eyed maiden, I came from the northern border of the country. If I seem rude in demanding so much service, I do hereby offer my regrets. Nothing would distress me more than overburdening the golden-lotus feet and the snowy-jade palms of your exquisite self.

FONG FONG. An humble maid appreciates profoundly your lavish compliments. We shall call for the blessed help from the God of the Kitchen to fulfill your orders, and the wine-fairies to relieve your thirst. With your permission, I shall retire from your honorable presence to proceed with preparations for your thirty-course dinner.

CHENG TE. Not so hurriedly. Fair maiden, I have been so profusely feasted on your beauty that I have no desire to defile myself with earthly yieldings.

FONG FONG. Later, perhaps?

CHENG TE. Later, perhaps.

FONG FONG. Then there is nothing I can serve you now, Venerable Sir? (*She starts to go.*)

CHENG TE. Yes, there is... (*He rises and goes toward her.* FONG FONG *retreats.*)

SHIAO FONG (*without*). Fong Fong, come in here; what has been keeping you so long?

FONG FONG (*relieved to have found an excuse to leave*). Please give me leave to go. My humble brother will return to wait on you immediately.

CHENG TE. Will yourself return, presently?

FONG FONG. I will answer presently. (*She runs out, left.*)

CHENG TE (*looking after her*). It is deplorable that such a lovely plum blossom should be wasted thus.
(THE PROPERTY MAN *plays the flute as* THE EMPEROR'S ATTENDANT *appears stealthily at the right entrance. He pokes in his head, and sees* THE EMPEROR. *He gives a sigh of relief and surprise; then comes swiftly in, still on tiptoe. When he is face to face with* CHENG TE *he kneels and kowtows.*)

THE ATTENDANT. My Lord of Ten Thousand Years, at last I have found your Majesty. The Buddha be thanked! (*He kowtows again.*)

CHENG TE (*annoyed*). Why came you here? Is there any place on earth where we can enjoy peace and not be everlastingly disturbed by your findings?

THE ATTENDANT. Yes, Your Majesty, in the Forbidden Palace of Purple Peking. (*He rises.*)

CHENG TE. Dare you speak thus to your Emperor?

THE ATTENDANT (*kneeling again*). Your Majesty has been away from the Capital for more than nine-score days, longer than all Your Majesty's previous absences from the Forbidden City. The Governor of Chiangsi received an imperial command from Peking two days ago ordering him to make a thorough search in an attempt to find Your Majesty. There is suspicion that Your Majesty may be found near the town of Mai Lung. This conviction is based on the fact that the

Province of Chiangsi is the only province which has not been honored with Your Majesty's golden feet, and the town of Mai Lung in this province has been celebrated for years for its rice wine and (*With a twinkle in his eye.*) for its beauteous damsels! (CHENG TE *is annoyed but* THE ATTENDANT *does not notice this.*) How Your Majesty has missed this most attractive region is beyond anyone's comprehension. (CHENG TE *strikes the table and* THE ATTENDANT *checks himself and kowtows again.*) I crave Your Majesty's golden pardon; I deserve to die. (*He is trembling all over now.*)

CHENG TE (*amused*). What is your message then, if we may ask?

THE ATTENDANT. Ever since Your Majesty left the town of Ching Tan four days ago I have been tramping all over this province. Finally I traced Your Majesty to this tiny town of Mai Lung. I have—

CHENG TE (*impatient*). Did you say that they have been searching for us?

THE ATTENDANT. Yes, Your Majesty, in an unofficial and secret manner. My Lord of Ten Thousand Years, Your Majesty must leave for the Capital at once. The Capital cannot function well with her Emperor being absent for so long a season.

CHENG TE. Let me think ... (*Stroking his beard.*) We have some unfinished affairs to attend to, here. Return soon with our guards and wait outside for further instructions.

THE ATTENDANT. Yes, Your—(*Before he finishes* SHIAO FONG *comes in from the left.*)

SHIAO FONG. Ah-ya, another man! (THE ATTENDANT *is taken aback, and starts to go.*)

SHIAO FONG (*eagerly*). Your humble maid is at your service, Venerable Sir.

THE ATTENDANT. I need not your service.

SHIAO FONG (*assuming a business-like manner*). Will you please have a seat, sir?

THE ATTENDANT. I do not think I shall take a seat here. (*Glancing at* CHENG TE *and attempting to leave again.*)

SHIAO FONG. Venerable Sir, you must be thirsty. We have the most delicious rice wine. It is as clear as water— only it does not taste like water. If you are hungry, we will prepare for you genuine bird's-nest soup. And if you are looking for a lodging, you may stay with us— I mean you may stay, here in my brother's Inn.

THE ATTENDANT. I thank you profoundly. I am neither thirsty nor hungry, nor am I looking for lodging. Good-bye and thank you. (*He tries to leave once more.*)

SHIAO FONG (*perturbed*). Then why did you come in here? Know you not that this is my brother's Inn? State your true intentions and I will judge whether or not I will report you to the local magistrate.

THE ATTENDANT. I—I—did have some intentions when I first came but—I—I—do not have any now.

SHIAO FONG. You mean that your intentions vanished when you saw the place, or after you had seen some one in this place. (*Meaning herself, hurt and offended.*)

THE ATTENDANT. Yes—no. I did not see anyone! I mean —yes, I did see someone. But—I—you (*Confused when he becomes conscious that his* EMPEROR *has been watching him all the time.*) With your permission I must take my leave now. (*He hurries away while* THE PROPERTY MAN *plays the flute to accompany his exit.* SHIAO FONG *watches him go, sighing softly.* CHENG TE *watches the scene indulgently and is greatly amused.*)

CHENG TE. Waste not your precious sighs on such an unworthy soul. Sighs are our hearts' fond confessions, especially those silently uttered from a maiden's lips. Beware, my fastidious maiden, sighs are treacherous. They betray our hearts.

SHIAO FONG (*she does not seem to have heard him*). Your orders, please, Honorable Sir.

CHENG TE. Ask your sister to come.

SHIAO FONG. I can wait on you equally well. Would you like some roast pigeon's eggs as one of your courses for dinner? They are delicious. And some rice wine? (*There is no response from* CHENG TE.) How do my suggestions appeal to you, Eminent Sir?

CHENG TE. Very slightly. (*Commandingly.*) Tell your sister I desire her presence at once.

SHIAO FONG (*frightened, she turns and calls*). Fong Fong, the gentleman wants you! (FONG FONG *enters from the left.*) Fong Fong, let me warn you, that man has dishonorable intentions. I see that on his face. Be cautious.

FONG FONG. Thank you, my sister. I shall not be carried away. Please do not worry your heart about me.

SHIAO FONG. Cry out if you need me. (SHIAO FONG *goes within by the left entrance.* FONG FONG *stands silent, while* CHENG TE *beats on the table again.*)

FONG FONG. Yes, your honorable.

CHENG TE. My patience has its limits. Are we or are we not going to have something to satisfy our thirst and hunger?

FONG FONG. I regret to say that it is not within my power to relieve you of your needs immediately. We have to wait for my humble brother's return.

CHENG TE. There is one thing which is definitely within your power.

FONG FONG (*puzzled*). Yes?

CHENG TE. Would you like to see Peking, the royal site of the Emperor Cheng Te and visit the Forbidden Palace?

FONG FONG. Me, see Peking? How ridiculous. How am I to go to see Peking, which is thousands of leagues away? A maiden never travels that far. It is unheard of.

CHENG TE. I shall bring you to the Capital if you will only allow me.

FONG FONG. Sir, I am a respectable girl from a highly respectable family, though we do operate an inn. Remember, my sister and I are not alone here. We have close neighbours who all have ears—very alert ears too. Beware what you say and do. If you do not act like a gentleman, there will be those here who will teach you how to behave.

CHENG TE. They will regret it if they attempt to do so. No one can teach The Emperor how to behave. Have you not learned that from the Book of Spring and Autumn?

FONG FONG. The Emperor? Emperor. (*Her breath stops in her throat.*) Then you are the Wandering Dragon that we have heard so much about in the legends— The Emperor in disguise who has been travelling all over the country in his search for a peony-wreathed Empress? So that is the meaning of my dream of last night. Merciful Buddha! My family is delivered from fire and famine, (THE PROPERTY MAN *hands her a cushion.*) and my heart is filled with relief and gratitude! (*Realizing now that she is in the presence of The Emperor, she kneels before him.*) Your August Majesty, with profound respect and trembling reverence I beseech you to pardon my rude behavior, to forgive my simple country manners, and to restore my humble self to your golden favor.

CHENG TE. What can we do for you, my lovely lotus blossom?

FONG FONG. Any gesture from your gracious self will be a heavenly blessing.

CHENG TE. Be our Empress and accompany us to Peking.

FONG FONG. Empress? Empress! (*She cannot believe her own ears.*) The Mistress of the Purple Palace? But—but, without the consent of my Reverend Mother? No, no, my August Lord, I cannot do that. The decision rests not in my hand.

CHENG TE (*rising*). We understand. (*Putting on his travelling cloak.*) Gentle maid, please see that my steed is ready. (*She hesitates a moment, then speaks.*)

FONG FONG. But, Sire, I trust Your Majesty is not withdrawing your former invitation? I hope you are not leaving without my humble company?

CHENG TE. The decision rests not in my hand. (SHIAO FONG *appears at the left entrance, and overhears them.*)

FONG FONG (*resolved*). I will pack my belongings presently. Do forgive me that I shall not be able to attend to your noble steed now. (*She smiles at him coquettishly.*)

CHENG TE (*delighted*). I would not think of letting you do it now. I shall attend to it myself.

SHIAO FONG. I must stop this! (*Hurrying out, left.*)
(CHENG TE *gazes at* FONG FONG *admiringly; she is embarrassed and runs out, left.* CHENG TE *follows her.* LEE MU *and* LEE LUNG *enter from the right, one in a carriage and the other on a donkey. They dismount and enter the Inn. They are greeted by* SHIAO FONG, *who is evidently in great distress.*)

SHIAO FONG (*even forgetting to bow to her mother*). Reverend Mother, we are in great distress.

LEE MU. What, our house on fire in spite of our incense and prayers?

SHIAO FONG. No, no. But Fong Fong is on the verge of eloping with a man, a stranger whom she waited on during the absence of our brother. Reverend Mother, you must stop her immediately.

LEE MU *and* LEE LUNG. What, Fong Fong going away with a man!

LEE MU (*almost fainting but recovering quickly*). She is bewitched! Fetch me a broom, we must dis-charm her and break the spell. Where are they? (THE PROPERTY MAN *brings her a broom.*)

SHIAO FONG. I think the man is outside attending to his horse. Brother, do something quickly.

LEE LUNG. I will stop them. (*Starting to go, but hesitating on a second thought.*) Is he armed? Let me call the neighbours first.

LEE MU. Stop, do not call the neighbours. Do we not have shame enough without shouting to everyone in town? (*She starts to go, left. LEE LUNG and SHIAO FONG follow her.*) I shall go and see them myself. What disgrace! How can I ever lift my head! (*To heaven.*) Punish them, Buddha, if you have eyes. Punish them. They have degraded themselves to the eighteenth depth of hell. Yen Wang, God of the Underworld, torture them on your Mountain of piercing swords and devour them with your wheel of scorching flames! Hounds and serpents of the Fifth King of Yen Lo Den, pursue them, and tear them into ten thousand

pieces. (*Weeping, she turns to her two children.*)
What shall I say to your father when I see him in
heaven?

LEE LUNG. Mother, curse them not. It will be of no avail.

LEE MU. I will curse them. I will curse them until my
flesh is rotted from my bones! But I will see *him* rot
in the grave first, the black heart! I will see him rot in
the grave.
(CHENG TE *enters from the left and* THE PROPERTY
MAN *hands him the whip, which he tosses to the
floor.*)

SHIAO FONG. Mother, this is the man!

LEE MU. So, *you*! You black heart of a hollow trunk,
you treacherous deceiver, you sorcerer! What have
you to do with my fair virgin daughter? I will plead
in the supreme court of His Majesty's Capital and
have you executed for witchcraft and... and...
(*Raising her broom.*)

CHENG TE. What gesture is this? That is too trying for
our tolerance. Royal guards!

THE ATTENDANT and THE GUARDS (*outside, loudly*).
Yes, Your Majesty. (THE PROPERTY MAN *strikes sev-
eral times on the great gong.* THE ATTENDANT *and*
TWO GUARDS *come running in from the right.*) Your
Majesty, Lord of Ten Thousand Years.

CHENG TE. We leave for the Capital immediately.

THE ATTENDANT and GUARDS. Yes, Your Majesty.

CHENG TE. Usher in the Empress from yonder chamber. She is now making her preparations to accompany us.

GUARD. Yes, Your Majesty. (*Bowing, they leave by the left entrance.*)
(THE ATTENDANT *helps* CHENG TE *don his travelling cloak.*)

LEE MU (*overwhelmed, kneels*). Your Majesty, my Lord of Ten Thousand Years, my August Sire, my Royal Emperor...I...I...deserve to die... (*She weeps.* SHIAO FONG *and* LEE LUNG *kneel beside her. She passes the broom to* LEE LUNG *and he hurriedly returns it to* THE PROPERTY MAN.)

FONG FONG (*comes in, followed by* A GUARD. *She kneels*). I beg that Your Majesty's gracious pardon be extended to my poor, humble mother.

CHENG TE. We shall all proceed to Peking.

LEE MU (*incredulously*). Including my humble self and my two other children?

CHENG TE (*casually*). You have our pardon.
(CHENG TE *leaves the Inn,* THE ATTENDANT *taking up the whip and helping him to mount his horse. The others rise and prepare to leave.* THE PROPERTY MAN *supplies two carriages, one for* FONG FONG *and one for* LEE MU *and* SHIAO FONG. *The* TWO GUARDS *serve as carriage-men.*)

LEE LUNG (*reluctantly following the others*). Reverend Mother, we cannot leave now. What will become of the wedding?

LEE MU. What wedding?

LEE LUNG. My wedding with the maiden Chao.

LEE MU. No, no wedding for you now. We shall go to Peking and there I shall select from all the lovely maidens the most beautiful one for you. Know you not that you are now His Majesty's Mother-in-Law's son?

LEE LUNG (*following her out*). But mother, I am contented and happy with the lovely Chao. Please, mother, please!

THE GUARDS (*shouting*). Silence! Silence! Silence! Clear the way for His Majesty, The Emperor! Clear the way for His Majesty, Lord of Ten Thousand Years!
(THE PROPERTY MAN *strikes the drum and* THE GOD *and* GODDESS OF EARTH *appear*.)

THE GOD and GODDESS OF EARTH (*bowing deeply*). Farewell to Your Majesty.

CURTAIN

CANADA

THE COURTING OF MARIE JENVRIN

BY *Gwen Pharis*

THE CHARACTERS

*As originally produced by the Banff School of Fine
Arts of the University of Alberta on their Fifth Bill of
Experimental Productions of New Canadian Plays,
August 25 and 27, 1941. First published in* THE CARO-
LINA PLAY-BOOK *for December, 1941.*

MR. WERNECKE,
    proprietor of the Beaverlodge Hotel . . . . John Hickey
MRS. WERNECKE, *his wife* . . . . Beatrice Curotte
MARIE JENVRIN . . . . Margaret Vavra
LOUIS HEBERT, *a young miner* . . . . Jim Linn
FATHER LEBEAU, *a flying priest* . . . . . . Vanick Galstaun
MR. DINSMORE, *a business man* . . . . Jack Sheinin
MICHAEL LORRIGAN, *a miner* . . . . Glenn Wilms

THE SCENE: The combined lunchroom and sitting-
room of the Beaverlodge Hotel in Yellowknife, North
West Territories, Canada.

THE TIME: The present. A late afternoon in February.

THE SCENE

The curtain rises on the combined lunchroom and sitting-room of the Beaverlodge Hotel in Yellowknife, North West Territories. A bear rug on the floor, a mounted caribou head, some heavily-beaded mukluks [1] of Indian fashion, and a man's parka [2] with heavily-furred hood—this last hanging near the door—are some tangible evidence of the Northern setting. Less colorful but essential furniture in the room includes a good-sized wood or oil heater at the left, two old leather armchairs, a small stand-table for magazines and papers, a table with three painted chairs grouped round it, and a narrow counter at the right with three or four wooden stools in front of it. In the rear wall two windows and a door look out on the main street of the mining town. Up left is a door leading to the rooms upstairs and down right is a door that leads outside through the kitchen.

Our first glimpse of life in the Beaverlodge Hotel comes at about 3:30 on a February afternoon. Darkness comes early in the North, and the shadows are deepening in the room. It is a slack time, since the miners do not come off shift until after 4 o'clock.

We discover a rather apologetic-looking little man seated on the floor in front of the large chair right of the stove, surrounded by three pulp magazines and a strange assortment of screws, coils, and machinery, the

1. Knee-high buckskin or caribou boots like moccasins, often elaborately trimmed with fur, embroidery, or bead work.
2. A long heavy woolen coat with a hood attached.

*largest piece looking much like a food-chopper. In the
armchair left of the stove a large, placid-looking woman
with the rather gaudy beauty of a great sunflower is
dozing peacefully, a box of chocolates beside her. These
good people are* MR. *and* MRS. WERNECKE, *proprietors
of the Inn. Behind the counter, folding paper napkins
and tidying the cigarette and gum boxes on the shelf, is*
MARIE JENVRIN.

MARIE JENVRIN *is perhaps nineteen, with a vivid little
face, framed by dark, curly hair. She wears a flared skirt,
a blouse graced with a demure little collar, and tiny bow
tie. Around her waist is a flared apron as gay as fancy can
conceive.*

MR. WERNECKE *is muttering to himself as he ecstati-
cally assembles his machinery.*

WERNECKE. She won't fit. His directions is wrong. (*He
refers to one of the magazines.*) He says it fits but I
make it and it don't fit. (*He takes up the paper and
addresses it politely.*) Your directions are just plain
damn wrong, Mr. Beasley. You don't ought to publish
such directions.

MARIE. You work at a new invention, *Monsieur?*

WERNECKE. Yes, Marie, but that Beasley makes a mistake. (*The light dawns.*) Wait! No, he don't! She fits.
I have the wrong side. See, now she fits perfect. (*He
holds up a coil which fits inside a circle of steel.*)

MARIE. *C'est bon.* What is this—invention, *Monsieur?*

WERNECKE. Ah, a surprise! You will know tomorrow. I
have one more part to come in by the plane.

MARIE. I think the plane does not get in after all. It is 3:30 and getting dark. The storm has kept him.

WERNECKE. If it is BQQ it will not come. If it is BVY it will come—you see. That BQQ is a bad plane. She looks good but she won't go. I don't like that BQQ. Twice I have been held up on an invention, waiting for that plane.

ANNABELLA (MRS. WERNECKE) (*stirring drowsily*). Fiddlesticks. I have gone outside in both. BQQ is better. I don't get sick in BQQ.

WERNECKE. Women don't know about aeroplanes. She looks nice so you think she is nice. I tell you BQQ is no good. (*To himself.*) She's a *bidget!*

ANNABELLA (*sharply*). What's that you say, Wernecke?

WERNECKE (*slightly belligerent*). I said, Mrs. Wernecke, that BQQ is a *bidget*. That's a word I invented.

ANNABELLA (*taking a chocolate*). Well, I don't like it.

WERNECKE (*going back to work*). That is too bad. I like it. (ANNABELLA *is too sleepy to continue the argument.*)

MARIE (*taking a glass of paper napkins over to the table*). Father LeBeau was to come in today. I hope the storm has not forced them down and they have lost themselves.

WERNECKE. No need to worry about the Father, Marie. He knows the North from McMurray to Aklavik. He has gone down to Aklavik alone with three dogs.

MARIE (*at the window*). Louis Hébert stands on the aeroplane dock. How foolish to stand shivering in such cold.

WERNECKE. Perhaps while Father LeBeau is here you will marry with Louis, Marie.

MARIE (*turning from the window and beginning to light the lamp on the table*). And perhaps I will not, Monsieur. I have no mind to marry Louis Hébert.

WERNECKE. Then what of Ed McArthy or William Shumlett or Michael Lorrigan?

MARIE. Michael Lorrigan! Such a man! *Non*, Monsieur Wernecke, I prefer to work in your hotel, please.

ANNABELLA. We will give Father LeBeau the green room. It is warmer.

WERNECKE. He can have his choice of rooms—if he comes.

ANNABELLA. Well, he must come some time. If not today, tomorrow.

WERNECKE. If it is BQQ I shall not be surprised if he never comes. (*The droning of a plane is heard quite close.*)

MARIE (*excitedly*). *Écoutez!* The plane! I hear it. (*They all listen. Their faces light up.*)
(*Now the engine of the plane can be heard distinctly. All three are excited and hurry toward the window. MR. WERNECKE takes time to thrust his invention into*

a box, which he pushes under the table. Their voices rise with pleasure.)

WERNECKE *(gathering up his invention)*. It is a plane! BVY has come through the storm.

MARIE. There it is! See, *Madame*. He circles above the bay.

ANNABELLA. It is dark to land.

WERNECKE. Hah! That BVY can land any place.

MARIE. Michael Lorrigan says the ice is not safe by the Hudson Bay dock. There is a current there.

WERNECKE. It is time a plane got in. Now I can finish my invention. *(He comes to the window where the women are watching.)*

ANNABELLA. My new silk dress will be on it—and slippers for Wernecke.

MARIE. *Oui, et une lettre de ma mère.*

WERNECKE. He brings her down fast. No nonsense. I like to see a good plane brought down fast.

MARIE. *Attention!* He is about to land.

ANNABELLA. That is BQQ or I am not Annabella.

MARIE. I think you are right, Madame. *Voilà*—he is on the ice. That is a good landing. He is on the ice and no bumps.

ANNABELLA (*triumphantly*). And it is BQQ. I can see from here. So, Wernecke, BQQ cannot come in a storm.

WERNECKE. There is some mistake. I could swear it was the other.

ANNABELLA. Now what have you to say?

WERNECKE (*with dignity as he dons his parka*). I say nothing. I go to meet the guests. If it is BQQ, I expect no guests—they have probably fallen out the bottom.

ANNABELLA. What stubbornness! Soon you must invent an aeroplane, I suppose.

WERNECKE. I have thought of it.

ANNABELLA. Now, hurry, Wernecke. They will be getting out in a minute.

WERNECKE. They can get out without me, Mrs. Wernecke. (*With offended dignity, he leaves.*)

MARIE. Father LeBeau has come. I see him.

ANNABELLA. Shaking hands with the Mounted Policeman.

MARIE. And there is Madame Barnett. Her husband and little girl are kissing her.

ANNABELLA. Marie, isn't that Mr. Dinsmore—getting off now?

MARIE. *Ma foi*, he only went outside last week.

ANNABELLA. He's a queer one. I wonder where he makes his money. Certainly not in that jewelry store of his.

MARIE. It takes much money to fly back and forth so often.

ANNABELLA. Michael Lorrigan says he's a crook.

MARIE. There is someone else. Oh, it is only Louis talking to the pilot. Now he is running up here. (*Giggling a little.*) Wherever he goes, Louis must run like a scared rabbit.

ANNABELLA. I'd better go up and make sure the green room is ready.

MARIE. And I must finish my pie.
(*They turn from the window.* ANNABELLA *takes a chocolate as she starts upstairs.*)

ANNABELLA. Why don't you eat a chocolate, Marie? Michael left them for you.

MARIE. I do not eat chocolate. Besides, how do I know he leaves them for me?

ANNABELLA. I suppose a handsome young miner leaves chocolates about for Mrs. Wernecke.

MARIE. Michael Lorrigan speaks only insults. No man can speak insults to Marie Jenvrin.

ANNABELLA (*placidly as she lumbers upstairs*). Pride falls, Marie, pride falls. I was like you once. Now, as you see, I am a slave to Wernecke. (*She goes off.*)

MARIE (*patting the caribou head affectionately*). Such foolishness they talk, *mon petit*. As if Marie must marry tomorrow or be forever left.

(MARIE *moves behind the counter. As she begins rolling out a pie crust which is already mixed,* LOUIS HEBERT *pokes his head in cautiously through the door at back.* LOUIS HEBERT *is a dapper young man, not very tall, dark and rather good-looking. He is excitable and far from levelheaded. The romance of the North is in his soul only as far as clothes are concerned. He wears a heavily-furred parka, elaborately embroidered mitts, and mukluks with huge red tassels, and is indeed a colorful sight.*)

LOUIS. Marie! Are you there? I bring you something.

MARIE. Of course I am here, Louis Hébert. Don't you see me?

LOUIS (*coming into the room*). Marie, do you know what day this is?

MARIE. Tuesday, *mon petit chou!*

LOUIS. Ah, but is something else, also. February 14—that is Saint Valentine's. And I have sent to Edmonton for a valentine for Marie Jenvrin. It comes by the aeroplane. (*He presents her with a large red envelope.*)

MARIE. You should not spend your money on me, Louis.

LOUIS. Aren't you going to open it?

MARIE (*as she opens it*). It is a very big valentine. So much lace and ribbon.

Louis (*unable to wait for her to open it, he takes it from her*). Look, this is best of all. When you open this little red heart—there is my picture. *Voilà!* (*He demonstrates.*)

Marie (*with a little throaty giggle*). *Oui*, it is you all right and looking very solemn.

Louis. You like it, Marie?

Marie. *Mais oui, c'est beau*. But, Louis, you should not give it to me. I am not your valentine.

Louis. Marie, could you not love me a little bit? Louis Hébert would serve you like a slave. Even when you are angry you are beautiful, Marie. In my mind I call you *La Belle du Nord*.

Marie. Your tongue says fine things, Louis. No wonder Cécile Rideau lies awake weeping for love of you.

Louis. Cécile Rideau!

Marie. Go to her, Louis. Have I not said a hundred times —four hundred times—I will not marry you?

Louis. If I fall down the mine shaft or get eaten up by huskies, you will be sorry then.

Marie (*returning to her pie*). No man gets eaten up by huskies for love, Louis Hébert. Only for lack of brains.

Louis. Two years I stay in this wild country of rock only because of you, Marie. Two years I work in the mine. Two years I set myself down on the shore of a lake, one thousand miles from any place. And no way to get out except by those aeroplane which make me so sick. And still you do not love me!

MARIE. When the ice melts there will be a boat. You can go outside then.

LOUIS. What is outside for me if you are not there? *Non*, if you must stay by this frozen lake beside the North Pole, then Louis Hébert stays too.

MARIE. Louis, Louis, it is no use. I will never love you— not for all the gold in Yellowknife.

LOUIS. I know—I am what they call—a dope. But I stay.

MARIE. *Très bien*. If you must stay, you stay. But what if I tell you there is a whisper of love—just a small stirring—in my heart for someone else?

LOUIS. I will fight him.

MARIE. *C'est impossible*. Besides, he does not love me.

LOUIS. Then he is a fool with no eyes. I can fight him.

MARIE. He is twice as big as you. Anyway, perhaps I do not love him. Perhaps I hate him. *Mais, j'ai mal au coeur*, Louis.

LOUIS (*solemnly*). *Moi, aussi*. We French suffer, Marie.

MARIE (*with a big sigh*). *Oui, nous souffrons*. (*For a brief period these very young people suffer. Then* MARIE *turns briskly back to her pie.*) There, it is ready for the oven. See how beautiful, Louis.

LOUIS. You are wonderful.

MARIE (*complacently*). I make good pies. Outside where I have cream to pile on top, I take prizes for my pie. But enough talk. Be a good boy and go down to the lake and bring me two pails of water.

LOUIS. Every day I cut holes in the ice to bring you water.

MARIE. I know, Louis. (*She smiles at him.*) You are very good, *mon cher.*
(*She hands him the pails, but before he leaves* MR. WERNECKE *enters with* FATHER LEBEAU. FATHER LEBEAU *is a rosy little priest with twinkling eyes.*)

MARIE. Père LeBeau! *Vous êtes ici.* (*She runs to him and gives him both her hands.*)

FATHER LEBEAU. Marie—Louis. *Comment allez-vous, mes enfants?* Marie grows prettier each week, *n'est-ce pas,* Louis?
(*He pats her cheek and shakes hands with* LOUIS.)

MARIE (*her eyes shining*). *C'est vous à la fin, mon père.* We are so glad to see you.

LOUIS. *Oui,* it is good to have you here, Père LeBeau.

FATHER LEBEAU. Your welcome warms my heart, my children. Now I will take my things upstairs—but I will be down again soon to eat one of your fine pies, Marie.

WERNECKE. I will lead the way, Father.

FATHER LeBeau. Thank you, Mr. Wernecke. This hotel always seems like home to me.

WERNECKE. I am honored, Father.

FATHER LeBeau. Have you been inventing lately?

WERNECKE. A new one—a surprise. See, the last part came in with you. (*He displays the treasured parcel.*)

FATHER LeBeau. I shall be glad to see it. (*They go upstairs.*)

LOUIS (*once more taking up his water pails*). Père LeBeau is here. There are rings at Dinsmore's. If you loved me, Marie, we could marry. As it is I am as lonely as—(*He searches for a simile.*)—as one rabbit's track in the snow. (*He adjusts his parka hood, pulls on his fine mitts, and is about to leave when* R. S. DINSMORE *enters from the street.* R. S. DINSMORE, *jeweler, is a stocky gentleman with an unctuous manner and sharp, suspicious eyes. He wears a large fur coat.*)

DINSMORE. Well, well, get two Frenchies together and the talk flies like crows in a cornfield. How are you behaving yourself, Miss Jenvrin?

MARIE (*coldly*). Did you wish something, *Monsieur?*

DINSMORE. Only to see old Wernecke. No hurry. (*He shakes the snow off his coat carelessly.*)

LOUIS (*without warmth*). You were not long in Edmonton.

DINSMORE. Just a little business trip, my boy. Some of us have to keep a foot on the ladder, you know.

LOUIS (*as he goes out the door*). You should take care you make no false steps, *Monsieur*.

DINSMORE (*after* LOUIS *has shut the door*). I see you've got your boy-friend working.

MARIE (*ignoring the remark*). Monsieur Wernecke should be down very soon.

DINSMORE. I can wait. Would you care to take a little walk after you're through tonight?

MARIE. A walk? What for?

DINSMORE. Why—just a walk—over to my shop maybe. To get out.

MARIE. I have been out. When I walk in twenty below zero, I have a purpose.

DINSMORE. Perhaps you'd like to see the moving picture?

MARIE. Thank you, *Monsieur*, you will excuse me but I do not care to go.

DINSMORE. As you like. You know, Miss Jenvrin, I've been thinking of opening a restaurant here. With your help the restaurant would become a very paying proposition.

MARIE. I have no wish to change jobs, *Monsieur*.

DINSMORE. You don't understand. You see, I'm a man of some means. I realize my position may seem rather out of reach to you, but I've been keeping my eye on you this last three months and—
(MICHAEL LORRIGAN *enters from outside. He is a tall, homely, and thoroughly attractive young man of great vitality.*)

MICHAEL. Well, Marie Jenvrin, have you a kiss for Michael Lorrigan, the hardest working hard-rock miner in the town of Yellowknife? On second thought I'll not kiss you. You've painted your mouth like a signboard. I'll have a cup of coffee instead.

MARIE. You'll have no kiss from me, Michael Lorrigan, and you pay for your coffee.

MICHAEL. Ten cents for cold coffee. No wonder I must go around in a ragged shirt.

DINSMORE (*turning*). Look here, my good man, you're interrupting—

MICHAEL. The name's Lorrigan, Mr. Dinsmore, and I'm nobody's man but my own.

DINSMORE. Prickly today, aren't you?

MICHAEL. I've been waiting for you to get back.

DINSMORE. Really?

MICHAEL. I understand you lent old Carl Swanson money to pay his poker debts, after getting him that drunk he didn't know what he was doing. He's been drunk ever since, but I got that much out of him.

DINSMORE. I lent him the money. Poor old codger. He shouldn't have sat in on a game with that bunch down at Joe's. They cleaned him.

MICHAEL. Did you take any security?

DINSMORE. Don't be funny. What security has Swanson got to give?

MICHAEL. I wouldn't know, Mr. Dinsmore, but I think you might. Carl keeps jabbering about some paper he signed.

DINSMORE. Oh, that, it's nothing. Tell him to come in and see me. I'll explain it to him in words of one syllable.

MICHAEL. He's soberin' up in my room now.

DINSMORE. Pleasant friends he has, eh, Miss Jenvrin?

MICHAEL. I wouldn't like to see old Carl cheated, Mr. Dinsmore.

DINSMORE. Tell him to keep away from the crowd that hang around Joe's, then.

MICHAEL. I'll tell him that—from you.

DINSMORE. Look here, Lorrigan, I felt sorry for the old soak. I lent him some money. What's the matter with that?

MICHAEL. If you did it out of kindness, I'll beg your pardon, Mr. Dinsmore. If not—(*He breaks off, puts a coin on the table, and speaks to* Marie, *turning away from* Dinsmore.) I did your coffee an injustice, Colleen. It's lukewarm. You're doin' better.

Marie. There is your change. You are welcome to go now.
(Michael *lights a cigarette and gazes nonchalantly at the smoke rings which he blows at the ceiling.*)

Michael. I was just thinking—

Marie. There is small use digging for gold where no gold is, *Monsieur.*

Michael. You'd be almost a pretty girl, Marie, if you controlled your tongue. Your nose is snub, of course, and there's too much red stuff on your lips, but you'd get by, if you didn't talk. Too bad. (*He shakes his head.*)
(Mr. *and* Mrs. Wernecke *come downstairs and into the room, arguing vociferously.* Annabella *carries a tall, rangy plant.*)

Annabella. I tell you, Wernecke, it is the B 1 tablets that have made this begonia plant grow.

Wernecke. B 1! The plant was withering away to a shadow until I invented my plant food—all its growing is because of my plant food.

Annabella. Nonsense! Your plant food didn't help the geraniums. They died. B 1 is necessary to plant life.

Wernecke (*irritated*). B 1 be damned, Mrs. Wernecke. My plant food has made the begonia blossom like the pines of Lebanon. Am I right, Marie?

MARIE. Perhaps it is the soil Louis brings me for my garden that makes the begonia grow so tall.

ANNABELLA. Michael. I appeal to you—I read about B 1 and I try it. Immediately this plant shoots up two feet. Now Wernecke claims all the glory for his plant food. It is unreasonable!

WERNECKE. Every time I invent an invention around here somebody makes slams. Give me that begonia— I'll throw it out the window!

ANNABELLA. So, indeed! I will put it in my own sitting-room where you can't ruin it with your plant food. Credit taker! (*She glares at him, then takes a choco-late.*)

MICHAEL (*getting up*). Plant food alone cannot account for this wonderful plant, Mrs. Wernecke. B 1 alone might account for half of it. It is the combination. I am going upstairs. I'll leave it in your sitting room.
(*With a courtly smile,* MICHAEL *relieves* MRS. WER-NECKE *of the begonia plant.*)

ANNABELLA (*noticing that* WERNECKE *is grimly starting upstairs with his box*). Where are you taking that?

WERNECKE. To the green room. Intelligent people, like Father LeBeau, are interested—very interested in the things I invent. (ANNABELLA *gives an elaborate sniff.*)

DINSMORE. I don't suppose you could spare a minute from plant foods and such junk to rent me a room, Wernecke. No time for business, I guess.

ANNABELLA (*between chocolates*). The yellow room is ready, Wernecke.

WERNECKE (*pausing at the foot of the stairs*). I'm sorry. I have no rooms.

ANNABELLA. Why, Wernecke!

WERNECKE (*firmly, though it is an effort*). I have no room for Mr. Dinsmore.

ANNABELLA. Wernecke, the yellow room—

WERNECKE (*politely*). I'm sorry. You will have to go elsewhere.

DINSMORE. Look here, everybody knows you are not full. That priest and I were the only—

WERNECKE. I own this hotel. Perhaps everybody does not know that.

DINSMORE. Why won't you give me a room?

WERNECKE (*advancing and speaking in a very gentle voice*). Well, I will tell you. I just don't like you, Mr. Dinsmore. I never have liked you. I never will like you. So, when you ask me for a room, I suddenly decide I have no rooms. Now you know as much about it as I do.

ANNABELLA. Why, Wernecke, you've never acted like this before.

WERNECKE. I know. It surprises me too.

DINSMORE (*belligerently*). I suppose I can't eat in your lunch room?

WERNECKE (*considering*). Yes, you may have your supper here.

ANNABELLA. Wernecke, are you quite well?

WERNECKE. Quite well, Annabella, thank you. You will excuse me, Mr. Dinsmore. (*With a little bow he goes through the door leading upstairs.*)

ANNABELLA (*solemnly*). You shouldn't have called his invention junk, Mr. Dinsmore. He will be a great man some day. Inventing is a passion with him—a pure passion.

DINSMORE. What a hotel! What a way to run a business! I'll take away every customer—
(MICHAEL *reappears from upstairs.*)

MICHAEL. Well, the begonia plant is safe in your sitting room, Mrs. Wernecke. I put it in the window.

ANNABELLA. Ah! There is a draft in that window. It will freeze. Excuse me, sir. (*She brushes past* DINSMORE *and hurries out.*)

MICHAEL. Are you fond of begonias, Marie? (*He gets in her way.*)

MARIE (*moving to the table with two glasses of water*). Of course. But I am not fond of people who waste my time. *Allez!* (*She places the water on the table.*)

MICHAEL (*in a startled tone*). Marie, let me see the backs of your hands—quick.
(*Obediently* MARIE *extends her hands, palms down, lifting startled eyes to his. With a flourish,* MICHAEL *places a glass of water on each hand and walks off whistling "They're hanging Danny Deever.*")

MARIE. *Vous êtes un diable!* Take them off, you hear. Take them off at once.

MICHAEL. Never act without thinking, my pet. You can take my advice as that of an uncle.

MARIE. Better I have advice from that stuffed caribou! Take them off, I tell you—

DINSMORE. Permit me, Miss Jenvrin. (*He removes the glasses.*) A poor joke, sir.

MARIE. Thank you. Go now, Michael Lorrigan, or I will throw the kettle at you.

MICHAEL. 'Twould do less damage than one of your pies, my sweet.

MARIE. You dare! I win prizes for my pies—many times.

MICHAEL. Still, if I want good pie I go to the Chinaman's down the street.

MARIE. *Mon Dieu,* listen to him! If I had beautiful, fresh cream from the cow, *Monsieur,* I could make a pie that would set you dreaming of heaven. And a dream is as near as you will get.

MICHAEL. Cream! Listen to her! You're lucky to have cream in tin cans.

MARIE. That! It tastes like gasoline.

MICHAEL. Perhaps you think they should fly a cow in here for you, my grand lady. That's one thing even you can't have while you stay in the North, little Buttercup.

MARIE. So, you know everything. I could have a cow next week.

MICHAEL. Indeed! Could you now? (LOUIS HEBERT *enters with his pails of water.*) Hear that, Louis. Marie Jenvrin can have a cow flown in!

LOUIS. You are only talking, Marie.

MARIE. *Fermez la bouche*, Louis Hébert.

LOUIS. If you would marry me, we could go outside and Louis Hébert would buy you a cow.

MICHAEL. A grand idea. Marry Louis and go outside!

MARIE (*goaded beyond all reason*). Marry, marry, marry! I am sick of this talk about marriage. I will marry the man who brings me a cow on the noose to that door there, and no other. I swear it! Now, there is your answer. Get out, all of you!

LOUIS. Do you mean it, Marie—truly? About the cow?

MARIE. I have said it, haven't I?

DINSMORE. Foolishness. What would you feed a cow here?

MARIE. Carrots, *Monsieur*, that I raise in my garden.

DINSMORE. So, you have a garden? Very enterprising.

LOUIS. You bet. Marie is the true French *Canadienne*. Even in this god-forsaken rock she must have a garden. Seven of us carried dirt in pails from three miles to make a garden for Marie.

MICHAEL. I'm the only free man left in camp.

LOUIS. I will get the cow, Marie, and then we will marry and—

MICHAEL. You take the first plane out, Louis. Get yourself to a duck pond. The quacking would be restful after the clacking of her tongue.

LOUIS. You do not insult Marie! We will settle now.

MARIE. You do not, Louis. He would break you in two.

MICHAEL. Hold your whist, Marie Jenvrin. This is men's talk. (*To* LOUIS.) Forget it, Louis, I feel no malice toward you.

LOUIS. So, you will not fight. Very well. My honor is satisfied.

MARIE. I die of boredom with all this talk, talk, talk.

LOUIS. I am going now to the Canadian Airways, Marie, to see about the cow.

MARIE. Louis, I didn't mean—

LOUIS (*exuberantly*). A cow—you will see, it is nothing to Louis Hébert.

MARIE. But Louis—*attendez! Vous ne comprenez—*

MICHAEL. She's trying to tell you she didn't mean it, Louis. She talks only to fill silence—

MARIE. Who are you to know what I mean? Of course I mean it.

MICHAEL. I suppose then you'd put it in writing?

MARIE. Perhaps I would—

MICHAEL. And sign your name to it? Oh, no, my sweet, you are not that foolish!

MARIE. Foolish, is it? You think I could not have a cow. You think no man would care enough to buy a cow for Marie Jenvrin.

MICHAEL. Not even enough to buy a teeny weeny little calf. (*He measures a calf as big as a mouse.*)

LOUIS. I would, Marie.

MICHAEL. She was only joking, Louis. She knows you can't fly cows for nothing.

MARIE. Joking, was I? I will show you. (*To* DINSMORE.) Give me your pencil, *Monsieur.* (*He does so.*) Now, Michael Lorrigan, look with your eyes at this. (*She writes on the back of the valentine.*) "I, Marie Jenvrin, promise to marry the man who brings a cow to Yellow-knife to me.—Signed, Marie Jenvrin." What do you say now?

MICHAEL. You must have witnesses.

MARIE (*doubtfully*). And what are those?

DINSMORE. It makes it legal, Miss Jenvrin. See—I write witnessed by R. S. Dinsmore. (*He does so.*)

MICHAEL (*enjoying himself*). One is not enough.

MARIE. Write your name, Louis. (LOUIS *does so.*) So—I do not mean it, Monsieur Lorrigan. (*Triumphantly.*) Now it is—what you say? (*She turns to* DINSMORE.)

DINSMORE. Legal.

MARIE. That's it—legal. I will put it up here. (*She places it in a prominent place on the counter. To* MICHAEL.) I expect you feel very small now. (*She smiles contentedly; then with a sudden burst of anger leans toward him, measuring with her fingers.*) Like a teeny weeny calf, you feel small, I hope.

MICHAEL (*bursting into a roar of laughter*). Ah, Marie Jenvrin, you should listen to your Uncle Michael's advice. All the camp will hear of this. (*He goes over, gets a newspaper, and sits down to read.*)

LOUIS. I will order a Jersey cow, Marie. They have a very kind face. And a Jersey would fly best. They have good digestion.

MARIE (*crossly*). Always you talk too much, Louis.

LOUIS. Do not argue, *chérie*. (*He puts on his fine mitts.*) I know many brands of cow, and the Jersey, it is the kindest. *Au 'voir, mes amis.* (*He goes out in high spirits.*)

DINSMORE. What a fool! No wonder he wearies you, Marie.

MARIE. Speak no ill of Louis, *Monsieur*. He is my greatest friend.

DINSMORE. Excuse me. You know this business of the cow—it isn't so foolish as it first appears. There are children in this camp. Parents would pay fifty cents a quart for milk for their children. Some cows might be a good investment.

MICHAEL (*looking up from his paper*). You smell money like a rat smells cheese, Mr. Dinsmore. Milk for babes seems a little out of your line.

DINSMORE (*getting up*). Look here, Lorrigan, a man can express an opinion. You will excuse me, Marie. I'll be back later. (*He puts on his coat.*)

MARIE. Very well.

DINSMORE. Perhaps you will reconsider my invitation to the moving picture?

MARIE. Perhaps—in one hundred thousand leap years!

DINSMORE. These young girls must have their jokes, eh, Lorrigan?

MICHAEL. Be on your way, sir. Miss Jenvrin is busy.

DINSMORE. She is happiest when busy; I see that. And it is charming, Marie, charming. (*He goes out highly pleased with his compliment.*)

MICHAEL (*muttering to himself*). Blatherskite! A havering blatherskite.
(*There is a moment's silence while* MARIE *continues setting the table and* MICHAEL *reads his paper.* MARIE *takes up a heavy coal bucket and starts to put some in the stove.*)

MICHAEL (*angrily*). Here, you, put that down. (*He gets up and takes the heavy bucket from her.*) Have you no more sense than a daft mud-hen? (*He puts the coal in the stove as* MARIE *moves out of the way.*)

MARIE. To whom do you speak, *Monsieur?*

MICHAEL. To a lass who will sell herself for a cow on a noose—and because a poor Irish hard-rocker says her pie is not so good as the Chinaman's down the street.

MARIE. Keep your tongue to yourself, Michael Lorrigan. You are no more to me than—than a mouse in a field!

MICHAEL. Never mind, little bird. Perhaps old Dinsmore will have a fine cow flown in for you.

MARIE (*startled*). Oh, no—

MICHAEL (*returning to his chair*). Why not? He's pinched his ill-gotten pennies till he's squeezed dollars out of them.

MARIE. But, Michael, he's old—and there is greed in his face.

MICHAEL. Then I'll lend the money to Louis Hébert. You shall have your cow.

MARIE (*stung by his indifference*). To hear you boast of lending money is to hear wind in an empty chimney. Have I not heard how Michael Lorrigan gets drunk on a Saturday and gives his money to the Indians?

MICHAEL. Better an Indian papoose should have it than a French vixen!

MARIE. How dare you call names at me, Marie Jenvrin?

MICHAEL (*genuinely angry*). Who are you to say whether I can lend two hundred dollars or not? So, you think I'm a no-good wanderer with no thought for day after tomorrow. I'll show you. I'll lend the money to Black Oscar. Then you'll have to marry him and live in that dirty shack with eighteen huskies.

MARIE. I will marry whom I choose.

MICHAEL. Did you or did you not promise to marry the man who brings you a cow?

MARIE (*close to tears*). You drove me to it, by your insults.

MICHAEL. I thought it time you were taught a lesson. The world is not your oyster, my pretty goose.

MARIE (*shouting*). Take yourself out of the door! For a million dollars every day in golden money I wouldn't

have you around for an hour. You and your two
hundred dollars! Two hundred cents is more like it—
and that is more than you are worth!

MICHAEL (*at the door*). If I had two hundred dollars
and I have—I tell you, I wouldn't marry you if I got
a gold brick for a premium.

MARIE. Or I you for *two* gold bricks.
(FATHER LEBEAU *comes in. He looks at the two re-
proachfully.*)

FATHER LEBEAU. Children, children!

MARIE. He could do penance for twenty years, Father,
and not receive forgiveness for the wickedness of his
tongue.

MICHAEL. Have I or have I not two hundred dollars,
Father? Am I one to scatter money to the waves? Answer me that!

FATHER LEBEAU. Marie—Michael—This is no way. Control your—

MICHAEL. Control—I have not lost my temper in ten
years—but this, this—

MARIE. Make him go away, Father. How can you stand
up for him? He falls asleep at Mass; I've seen him.

MICHAEL. Don't worry, I'm going, and if I never come
back it is too soon. I mean soon enough. You hear me
—never!
(*He takes up his cap and miner's lamp and goes out.*)

MARIE (*following him*). Go, go, go! I would rather see the back of your heels than the face of a blessed angel!

FATHER LeBEAU (*as* MICHAEL *closes the door*). Marie, it is not good to get so angry.

MARIE. I am sorry, Father, if I blasphemed. (*She is very meek.*)

FATHER LeBEAU (*who has been looking at the document*). What is this? "I, Marie Jenvrin promise to marry ..." (*He reads the rest in silence.*) Marie!

MARIE (*a little frightened at his disapproval*). That Michael, Père LeBeau, he jokes about my pie, and I make a polite wish for cream and—

FATHER LeBEAU. It is not seemly to joke about marriage, Marie.

MARIE (*anxious to agree*). I know. You should talk gravely to that Michael, Father. He causes all this trouble. (*Almost ready to weep.*) Now I am in so much of a mix-up and all the camp will laugh at Marie Jenvrin. *C'est horrible!* Already Louis goes to get a cow. I wish to die.

FATHER LeBEAU (*smiling in spite of himself*). Louis would make a good husband.

MARIE. But I do not love him.

FATHER LeBEAU. What of Michael Lorrigan? He is a good man.

MARIE. To you, maybe. To me he is a werewolf in a sheepskin.

FATHER LeBEAU (*patting her shoulder*). Things may arrange themselves, my child. It costs much money to bring a cow by plane.

MARIE (*restored to cheerfulness*). Then you are not angry, *mon père?*

FATHER LeBEAU. No, Marie, but you must guard your tongue more carefully.
(LOUIS HEBERT *comes in, breathless and disconsolate.*)

LOUIS. Marie, you do not mean it about the cow. It costs two hundred dollars to fly one cow to this place. I have seventeen dollars, Marie.

MARIE (*smiling radiantly*). I would be a bad wife, Louis. I would throw things and lie in bed in the mornings.

LOUIS. What is it about a cow that you want so much?

MARIE. Cream, *mon petit chou*, cream. Do not feel bad, Louis. Cécile—why, I forgot to tell you—Cécile sends you a scarf. Madame Wernecke has it.

LOUIS (*stubbornly*). I do not wear it.

MARIE. What are you saying? Cécile has been knitting that scarf for two months. (*Smugly.*) Cécile is a very bad knitter, of course.

LOUIS (*mumbling*). Always you push, push, push me at Cécile Rideau. Sometime I will allow myself to be pushed. A man can't be strong of mind forever.

(*He is about to go upstairs as* MR. DINSMORE *comes in.*)

DINSMORE. Well, Louis, I hear you had some difficulty with your Jersey.

LOUIS (*crossly*). Your ears are too long, *Monsieur*.

DINSMORE. Better long ears than a short pocketbook, eh, Father LeBeau? (*He is very much pleased with himself.*)

LOUIS (*going out*). Scarves. I hate scarves!

DINSMORE. Marie, my girl, everything has been arranged for your satisfaction.

MARIE. I do not understand you, *Monsieur*.

DINSMORE. No need to be coy with me, young lady. You'll be in charge of the restaurant.

MARIE. You must be mad. I work in nobody's restaurant unless it pleases me.

DINSMORE. Of course not, until we are married.

MARIE. Married? I—marry *you?*

DINSMORE. I have paid the money and you are to have your cow. I wired for it to come on Monday. We will sell milk at fifty cents—

MARIE (*stricken*). You—you have bought a cow?

DINSMORE. To be flown in on the next plane. Two hundred dollars, it cost me, above the price of the cow, but we will soon make it up.

MARIE. Oh, no! Father—

DINSMORE. Two hundred dollars is a lot of money, but I am not worried.

MARIE. *Monsieur*, you did not understand. I was joking —I—

DINSMORE. I believe in striking while the iron's hot.

MARIE. *Monsieur*, you make a big mistake. I have no wish to marry.

FATHER LeBEAU. Surely you are not serious, Mr. Dinsmore. After all—

DINSMORE. Marie swore to marry the man who brings a cow to Yellowknife. I am doing this. We can be married on Tuesday.

MARIE (*frightened and pleading*). Please, *Monsieur*, it was a foolish vow. You would not want me for a wife. My temper—it is very bad.

DINSMORE. So was the first Mrs. Dinsmore's. Temper never bothers me. Perhaps you'd like to come in on Sunday to clean up our rooms a bit.

MARIE. Never.

DINSMORE. I've got an idea. I'll just run over to my shop and get you a ring—to wear until Tuesday.

MARIE. I won't have your ring.

DINSMORE. Now, now, no need to be foolish. We'll make our fortune, my girl, our fortune. (*He turns to go.*)
(MRS. WERNECKE *comes downstairs.*)

ANNABELLA. I'll give you a hand with supper, Marie.

DINSMORE. I've just done the Beaverlodge Hotel out of a good cook, Mrs. Wernecke. But to the victor the spoils, eh, Father? (*He goes out the door at the rear.*)

MARIE (*sinking down in a disconsolate heap*). Oh, I am so much a fool! *Qu'est-ce que je vais faire? Qu'est-ce que je vais faire?*

ANNABELLA. Marie, you are crying. What has happened?

MARIE. *Oh, je suis désolée. Je veux mourir.*

FATHER LEBEAU (*worried*). Come, Marie, you mustn't cry. We must think. You see, Mrs. Wernecke, Marie made a foolish vow to marry the man who brings her a cow—(*He hands* ANNABELLA *the document.*)

ANNABELLA. A cow? Here?

MARIE. And that Dinsmore has bought one. Oh, I wish to die, somewhere in the snow—alone!

FATHER LEBEAU. If only you hadn't signed a paper.

ANNABELLA. Don't cry, Marie. Wernecke is clever. He will help us.

MARIE. Nobody can help. I have nobody, nothing. I will be a prisoner in those awful rooms of Dinsmore's.

ANNABELLA. You shall not, Marie. Wernecke will—

MARIE. There is no time. Even now he brings me a ring. My heart is broken, broken.

FATHER LEBEAU. You might get into a rage, Marie, and throw things until he is frightened to marry you. (*Apologetically.*) It is only a suggestion—

MARIE. The vow is—what they call—legal. *Oh, mon coeur, mon coeur!*
(LOUIS *comes rushing in in great excitement, followed by* MR. WERNECKE.)

LOUIS. Marie! Monsieur Wernecke has invented the most beautiful, the most wonderful machinery. It is machinery to make cream! He gives it to me for you!

WERNECKE. That is the surprise, Marie.

LOUIS. Give me some canned milk and some butter. I will show you. Now we can be married, Marie. (*He waves the creammaker aloft.*)

WERNECKE (*as excited as* LOUIS). I make it from Mr. Beasley's directions.

LOUIS. He says you can't tell the cream from a cow's.

MARIE (*wailing*). Never say "cow" to me again. I hate cows. I wish they would never let any cow grow up to have horns.

WERNECKE. Marie—

LOUIS. *Ma belle*, you have tears—

ANNABELLA. Wernecke, read this. (*She hands him the paper.*)

LOUIS. Don't you want to see this machinery make cream, Marie?

MARIE. He talks of cream machinery, when my heart breaks. That is friendship.

WERNECKE (*puzzling over the document*). But I don't—

ANNABELLA. Dinsmore, Wernecke, Dinsmore is having a cow flown in. He wants to marry Marie.

LOUIS. Dinsmore! (*He looks tragically at* MARIE.) *Oh, ma petite!*

WERNECKE. Now I know why I don't like that man. We must stop this.

ANNABELLA. What can we do?

WERNECKE. I could dig a deep pit and cover it with snow. Then he would come along, just walking, and—

ANNABELLA. You can't dig pits in rock.

MARIE. I will take one dog and a sled and run away to the barren lands. I will not stop till I get to the northern lights.

LOUIS. You would freeze to death, Marie. That would be suicide. Nobody likes to commit suicide.

ANNABELLA. Are you sure this is legal?

MARIE. Two witnesses make it legal.

ANNABELLA. Maybe it doesn't. Louis, go upstairs and look in the Encyclopaedia. Find out what makes a thing legal.

LOUIS. I will. (*He runs over and kisses* MARIE's *hand.*) I will save you, Marie. (*As he goes.*) Louis Hebert will save you.
(DINSMORE *comes in from outside.*)

DINSMORE. Well, Marie, I have brought the ring. Come, my dear, give me your hand.

MARIE. No, no, I won't.

DINSMORE. It is a real diamond. Not one of the imitations.

MARIE. *Monsieur,* let kindness melt the rock of your heart. I do not want a ring or a cow or to get married. I want only to be left alone.

DINSMORE. I spend two hundred and fifty dollars on you and you refuse your part of the bargain. It is too late, my girl.

MARIE. You cannot force me to keep such a bargain.

DINSMORE. Can't I? I have bought the cow. That makes me your affianced husband.

MARIE. I will enter a convent.

DINSMORE. You will keep your promise or I will have a
lawsuit.

MARIE. Go away. I—I hate you!

WERNECKE. I warn you, I am inventing a way to stop
this.

DINSMORE. You and your inventions! I don't move a step
from here unless this woman keeps her bargain—or
pays me the two hundred and fifty dollars I have spent.
(MICHAEL LORRIGAN *comes in in a shining white shirt,
holding a magazine in his hand.*)

MARIE. Michael—

DINSMORE. Pay me the two hundred and fifty dollars or
marry me. That is your choice.

MARIE. But I never saw so much money.

DINSMORE. Then we will be married on Tuesday.

MICHAEL (*sternly*). What's this, Mr. Dinsmore? What
is your trouble?

DINSMORE. Trouble. I have no trouble. I bought this
woman a cow. Now she refuses to keep her bargain.
I'll take it to the law, I tell you.

MICHAEL. Just a minute, Mr. Dinsmore. I wouldn't be so
sure.

DINSMORE. You keep out of things that aren't your business. She marries me or pays me the money.

MARIE. Help me, Michael, don't make me marry him.

MICHAEL. But I thought you wanted to marry a man who would buy you a cow, Marie.

MARIE. It was my temper, Michael. Help me, please, Michael.

MICHAEL. You signed the paper, Marie.

MARIE. I didn't mean—

MICHAEL. And there were witnesses. To make it legal.

MARIE. I was only a foolish girl. I am suffering now. See, how I suffer.

MICHAEL. Still, this paper—

DINSMORE. I warn you, Miss Jenvrin, as he says—it is legal. You can't cheat me. Either you pay me the money or—

MICHAEL. Pay you nothing, Mr. Dinsmore. (*He tears up the document.*) That's enough!

DINSMORE. I'll take this to the law, I tell you.

MICHAEL. Listen, you black-hearted, tight-fisted, penny-pinching blackguard, you'll take nothing to the law. I've had my eye on you since you hit this camp. (*He puts his hand on* DINSMORE's *arm.*) You paid Carl

Swanson seventy-five dollars for a claim that may be worth thousands, and he so drunk he didn't know what he was signing. You'd be wise to hand over that paper to me now.

DINSMORE. What paper? I don't know what you're talking about.

MICHAEL (*tightening his grip*). No? Hand it over, Dinsmore. I'm not fooling.

DINSMORE. You've no right—(*He winces.*) All right, let go of me. (MICHAEL *releases him.*) There it is—for what it's worth. There's no gold on that claim.

MICHAEL. That's his business. Now you get out.

DINSMORE. I warn you, I'll have the law on you all. I'll see you in jail for this—

MICHAEL. You won't bother us again. You'll take the next plane out of here and stay out or you'll answer to me. And I'm the champion boxer in Great Bear Camp, Mr. Dinsmore.

DINSMORE. You can't do this. I'm a citizen of this—

MICHAEL (*suddenly picking him up and taking him to the door at the rear*). We can do with one less citizen like you. (*He tosses him out the door. Closing it, he returns nonchalantly.*) He made a big hole in the snowbank. Now, maybe I can read my paper in peace. (*He settles down comfortably by the fire.*)

MARIE. *Merci, mille fois, Monsieur.* You were very quick and very kind.

MICHAEL. Don't get ideas in your head. I threw him out on general principles and to save the claim of my friend, Carl Swanson, who when drunk has less brains even than Marie Jenvrin. Now, don't bother me, I'm reading.

FATHER LEBEAU (*sitting*). Well, I am quite exhausted. I'll soon be ready for some of your pie, Marie.

MICHAEL (*as if the subject had never come up before*). Say, Father, if you want good pie you ought to try Long Jim's. Best pie I ever ate.

MARIE. *Mon Dieu*, listen to him! I can't think—I cannot put on my lip rouge—I cannot speak English—I cannot cook—nothing I do is good—

MICHAEL (*calmly*). That's right. You're a bad-tempered, willful, spoiled brat with no mind of what you want. Crying for a cow like a baby for the moon. There's three hundred dollars. Now don't say Michael Lorrigan never saves any money. You buy your cow and live alone in your garden and frighten the children with your sputtering. (*He places a roll of bills on the counter before her.*)

MARIE. Three hundred dollars! You insult me with your money.

MICHAEL. I give it to you, with no strings attached— except peace from your havering.

MARIE. Oh, you are a—a—a devil! I call all the saints in heaven to see how I treat your money! (*She throws it at him.*) Take it, and take that, too, you—you—

blatherskite! (*She takes up a dipper of water and throws it over him.*)

ANNABELLA. Marie!

FATHER LeBEAU. Child, you mustn't.

MICHAEL (*very quietly*). So, you threw water on me. You spoiled my clean shirt that I ironed myself. All right, Marie Jenvrin. Now, none of you interfere, you understand?

MARIE. What are you going to do? I—I didn't mean—

MICHAEL. I'm going to give you something you've needed for a long time. I'm lucky to find a weapon at hand. (*He rolls up a magazine.*)

MARIE. Father!

FATHER LeBEAU. Michael, this is not—

MICHAEL. I said there's to be no interfering, Father. (*He takes up MARIE as if she were a flour sack and puts her over his knee.*) I'll give you twenty. One for each year. You can count them in French if you like. One! (*There is a resounding smack.*)

MARIE. Ouch! You let me go, Michael Lorrigan. Let me go. (*She kicks vigorously.*)

MICHAEL. Two, three, four, five.

MARIE. Ow! *Diable!* Father, he's hurting me. I'll bite your hand off.

MICHAEL. Six, seven, eight.

MARIE. *Mon Dieu*, he's killing me. You let him kill me!

MICHAEL. Nine, ten, eleven—Ouch, you vixen, would you take a piece out of my knee? Twelve, thirteen, fourteen.

MARIE. Enough, enough! I will never be angry again. I will—(*She beats on him.*) Fiend, Devil, put me down, I tell you!

MICHAEL. Fifteen, sixteen.
   (LOUIS HEBERT *comes in carrying a very large book.*)

LOUIS. The Encyclopaedia says—(*He stops short.*) Marie! (*He starts toward* MARIE *but* ANNABELLA *stops him.*)

ANNABELLA. No, Louis. Stay there.
   (LOUIS *starts to go on, but* FATHER LEBEAU *lays his hand on his shoulder.*)

FATHER LEBEAU. She is right, Louis. It is better so.

MICHAEL. Eighteen, nineteen, twenty. There! (*He sets* MARIE *on her feet.*) Now pick up that money and put it in a tidy roll.

MARIE (*in a small voice*). I won't.

MICHAEL. What's that you say?

MARIE. Yes, Michael. (*She kneels to take up the bills. There is a pause.*)

ANNABELLA (*suddenly decisive*). Wernecke, go and get the mail.

WERNECKE. Yes, Annabella. (*He goes quietly.*)

ANNABELLA. And Father, you and Louis must come up to see the begonia plant. It has grown so you wouldn't know it.

FATHER LeBEAU. Yes. It's amazing how the begonia plant grows, Mrs. Wernecke. (*He follows her toward the door.*)

ANNABELLA. Come, Louis.

LOUIS. Marie, do you want me to look at the begonia plant?

MARIE (*gently*). It is better so, Louis.

LOUIS. *Très bien*, Marie. I am—sorry. (LOUIS, *as he turns, starts winding a scarf around his neck.*)

MARIE. What is that on your neck, Louis?

LOUIS. It is the scarf that Cécile knit for me.

MARIE (*sadly*). *C'est bon.* You look very handsome. Cécile will be proud.

LOUIS. Father. Mrs. Wernecke. Wait for me. I come to look at the begonia. (*He follows the procession out sadly.*)
(*There is a painful pause.* MARIE *puts the money into a neat roll and tidies herself a little.* MICHAEL *continues to read.*)

MARIE (*in a very little voice*). I have picked up the money, Michael.

MICHAEL. Good.

MARIE. I feel very small. (*She measures.*)

MICHAEL (*without looking up*). Good.

MARIE. Michael—that spanking you gave me. It hurt me very bad.

MICHAEL (*still reading*). Very good.

MARIE (*drawing a little nearer, shyly*). Michael, was that —would you say that was the spanking of an—uncle?

MICHAEL (*looking at her doubtfully*). What else? What other kind of spanking would it be?

MARIE (*very small*). It is strange. I only thought—it reminds me so much of the spanking my sister Rose receives from her—husband.

MICHAEL. Indeed.

MARIE (*daring a quivering little smile*). It wouldn't be that kind, would it, Michael?

MICHAEL. And if it were? What would you have to say? (*He gets up and puts down his newspaper.*) Come here and tell me.

MARIE (*approaching a few steps*). I am here, Michael.

MICHAEL. Well! You're a small thing to cause a man's heart to flutter. But Michael Lorrigan is no coward. Look at me, Marie Jenvrin. (*He smiles at her as he tilts her chin up.*) Will we be getting married before the lenten season?

MARIE (*burying her head in his shoulder*). Michael! Michael, I'm crying.

MICHAEL. You've had a hard day. (*He dries her eyes with his handkerchief.*) Come, now. Shall we buy a cow with the money there?

MARIE. *Non, non.* I never want to see a cow! But Mr. Wernecke will make us a cream machine—and we will buy a little house with the money.

MICHAEL. 'Tis settled then. We'll tell Father tonight. One more thing; I'm to be boss in the household, Marie Jenvrin. There'll be no doubt of that. You understand. None of this "Michael this, and Michael that."

MARIE. *Oui*, I understand.

MICHAEL. Good. (*He kisses her lightly. Her hand goes up to trace his kiss as she looks at him.*)

MARIE (*with a sigh*). Michael.

MICHAEL. You're happy, Marie Jenvrin?

MARIE. I'm so happy. I could—(*She searches for words.*) I could eat up the sky! (*Breaking away.*) But it is near supper time. I must hurry.

MICHAEL. I'll get a fresh shirt. (*He turns to go.*)

MARIE. Michael, if it would not be—if you don't mind.
You see, the wood box—it is entirely empty. And it is
so late, I thought—

MICHAEL (*unaware of the web into which he has fallen*).
Sure, I'll fill it for you, Marie. No trouble at all.
(FATHER LeBeau *appears in the doorway. They do
not see him.* MARIE *runs to* MICHAEL *with the box. As
she gives it to him she lays her head against his shoulder
for a moment.*)

MARIE. You will be a wonderful husband, Michael. (*Her
eyes are shining as she looks into the future.*) I know
it!
(FATHER LeBeau *smiles benignly.*)

CURTAIN

MEXICO

THE RED VELVET GOAT

BY *Josephina Niggli*

THE CHARACTERS

As originally produced by The Carolina Playmakers on their Thirty-fourth Bill of Experimental Productions of New Plays in The Playmakers Theatre, Chapel Hill, North Carolina, October 31, 1935. First published in MEXICAN FOLK PLAYS, *by Josephina Niggli, published by The University of North Carolina Press, 1938.*

ESTEBAN .... Joseph Lee Brown
MARIANA, *his wife* .... Hester Barlow
LORENZO, *their son* .... Robert DuFour
ESTER, *a village girl* .... Barbara Hilton
LOLA } *friends of* ESTER .... { Jean Walker
CARMEN }   { Sarah Seawell
RAMON, *a peddler* .... Lawrence Wismer
DON PEPE,
    the mayor of The Three Marys ...... Wilbur Leech
DOÑA BERTA, *a neighbor* .... Gerd Bernhart
OTHER VILLAGERS .... Ralph Burgin, Eugene Langston,
    Raymond Staples, G. D. Gatling, Carl Anderson

THE SCENE: The patio of Esteban's home on the Street of the Arches in the town of The Three Marys.

THE TIME: Six o'clock of an afternoon in June, 1935.

THE SCENE

The late afternoon sun has thrown a golden haze over the patio of ESTEBAN'S *home. It is not a magnificent patio. There is no fountain with flowers banked around it, as in the home of* DON PEPE, *although there are pots of flowers on the stoop of the door which opens into a bedroom on the right. If it were noon, there would be chickens scratching about, and perhaps a baby pig or two, but it is evening, and the livestock have been closed up in the corral which is beyond the gate on the left.*

There are benches in front of us, and two rocking chairs swaying back and forth in front of a platform that is made of planks resting on saw-horses placed against the outside wall of the house at the back. This platform, these chairs, these benches are not usually found in ESTEBAN'S *patio, but they are here this afternoon because he is going to present a play of his own composition. The platform is in a very convenient place, since there is a door leading into the living-room which serves very well for the actors to make their entrances and exits. That funny little box in front of the platform is for the prompter, and those gray blankets dangling from the rope attached to the posts at the two front corners of the platform serve as curtains.*

To the left, now partly closed, is the great wooden door that opens directly on the street from the patio, and if you care to peer through the iron-barred window in the right wall you will see MARIANA'S *dress, which she intends to wear in her husband's play, laid out on the bed.*

The boy standing on the platform, clutching the stool in his two hands, is LORENZO, *very brown of eyes and skin and very black of hair. He wears the white pyjama suit of the tropics, with a red bandanna knotted at the throat. Because he is twenty-two, old enough to have a sweetheart, he has on a pair of bright yellow shoes that frankly hurt.*

That woman standing to the right with her hands buckled on her hips, that flaming, flashing woman is MARIANA, *his mother. Although she is forty there is no gray in the black satin cap of her hair; there are no wrinkles in the smooth golden cream of her skin; and as for her body ... well, even the loose white blouse and the billowing red muslin skirt cannot hide the youthful fire in that pretty body.*

It seems almost impossible to think of ESTEBAN, *the man leaning against the edge of the platform to the left ... it seems almost impossible to think of this funny, fat little man as being* MARIANA'S *husband. Sometimes he wakes up in the night, especially after feast days, and wonders himself how he ever came to marry such a gorgeous creature. Poor* ESTEBAN, *with his funny little blob of a nose perched in the middle of a round moon face, is no match for* MARIANA *and he knows it. His hands are always aimlessly clutching at each other. They are doing it now as he watches* LORENZO *with the stool.*

MARIANA (*impatiently to* LORENZO). No, fool! Where are your brains? Remove the chair and place it in the corner to the right. Esteban, speak! You are the master of the play.

ESTEBAN. To hear you rattle on, a man would think it was your scene. (*Points left.*) The stool goes there.

MARIANA (*points right*). No, there! Would you have it hide the door?

ESTEBAN (*angrily*). I say that it goes there! Lorenzo, place it where I say, or I will break your head!

LORENZO (*who, through the argument, has been standing still patiently holding the stool now bangs it down in front of him on the platform*). Holy saints! Whom am I to obey? I'll put it here, and you can change it where you like. I am an actor, not a doll on strings. I must go read my part again. (*Goes out through the platform door, slamming it behind him.*)
(MARIANA *hides a laugh.*)

MARIANA. He says he is an actor. Ha! Then I am queen of tragedy. What hour does it grow to be?

ESTEBAN (*taking a large gold watch from his pocket*). My watch says eight, so then it must be six. (*Bends toward her, clasping his hands tightly together.*) Does all the world know of the benefit?

MARIANA. Musicians played before each door in town. I sent Lorenzo out with notices this morning. Do you think our guests will pay enough to buy a goat? (*Sinks down on the end of one of the benches.*)

ESTEBAN. We only need ten pesos for a goat. Don Pepe said he'd sell us one of his. With the money from its milk and cheese we'll have enough to buy another one, and soon we'll have a flock. Then we'll be the richest two in town.

MARIANA (*scornfully*). Just with one goat? What silken dreams you can build from air. To hear you speak, no man in all the northern part of Mexico will be so rich as you when this play is done.

ESTEBAN (*with modest pride*). My talents are so varied, Mariana. Perhaps we should not buy a goat at all. Anyone can own a goat, but I, and I alone, can compose such drama.

MARIANA. A truth, a little truth indeed, my 'Steban. No other man could write such plays ... (*Flaring at him.*) ... because he would not write them. I think it best to buy the goat.

ESTEBAN (*shocked*). Have you no soul, no breath of genius blowing through your feeble brain? In time the world shall hear of this Esteban and mourn the fact that he possessed such a blockhead for a wife.

MARIANA (*peeved*). Who gave you hints of how to write it best but me, me, me! Who furnished you with chairs, and clothes, and men? Yes, men? (*Goes to him, her eyes burning with anger.*) Lorenzo is my son as much as yours. Oh, when I wept and cried the night that he made his first entry in the world I did not think that he would grow to be an actor.

ESTEBAN. Do not fear. My son has failed to grasp my talent. He—

MARIANA. Is better, far, than you will ever be.

ESTEBAN (*grandly ignoring her*). Did you bring the vase from Doña Berta's?

MARIANA. It is on the table in the house next to my red
and blue one. You see, I do not forget, even if you do.
(*Goes into the bedroom right.*)

ESTEBAN (*following her to the door and calling after
her*). Now what have I forgotten?

MARIANA (*from inside*). Just a prompter, that is all. (*She
enters, goes to the platform, and places the vases on
the prompter's box, standing back to see the effect.*) A
little prompter to aid us with his book when we forget.

ESTEBAN (*with a gasp*). I meant to ask Don Pepe—

MARIANA (*sarcastically*). Did you indeed? Don Pepe, the
mayor of The Three Marys! Perhaps you would prefer
to have the President of the Republic, or the great
civil judge to read our lines for us! Where are your
wits, fool? Hanging from your nose like Spanish moss
upon an ancient wind-blown tree?

ESTEBAN (*wringing his hands*). It grows near the hour of
our performance! Why did you not remind me of this
small detail?

MARIANA (*flings her arms above her head*). Remind you!
Saints in Heaven! Holy Mary aid me! Oh, what ass
is this dressed in man's clothing? Must I remember
everything? Or was the play of your invention?

ESTEBAN (*maliciously*). Who gave me hints of how to
write it? Who gave me chairs, and clothes, and men,
but you, my little, darling wife?

MARIANA (*furious*). But even I could not give you wit,
my love. Each day I watch your ears grow longer and

more pointed. Some day they will fall down and slap your cheeks, like that... (*Gives him a resounding slap.*) ... and then you will remember Mariana.

ESTEBAN (*ruefully*). You are the whip I wear here at my belt, my sweet—(*Rubs his face.*)—a whip that does not need my hand to wield its power.

MARIANA. Enough of arguments. The crowd will soon be here. Go out and hunt a prompter.

ESTEBAN (*scandalized*). At this hour? Have you no thought at all for my great art? Am I not the hero of this play? In a short time I must walk across that stage, and even now my poor heart is beating in my chest, and see my hands—(*Wiggles them loosely.*)—shaking at the wrist.

MARIANA (*firmly*). Am I not the tragic lady of this play? I will not speak a line of your great drama until a man is safe within that box.

ESTEBAN (*imploring aid from Heaven*). Why did I marry such a woman, who loves an argument more than her soul's salvation?

MARIANA (*also imploring Heaven*). Why did I marry such a lazy fool, who would rather sit in the sun and watch the goats feed on the mountainside than make an honest living for his family?
(LORENZO *opens the platform door and sticks his head through.*)

LORENZO. There are some people coming up the hill.

MARIANA (*giving a startled shriek. Runs toward bedroom door*). The audience! And I not dressed!

ESTEBAN (*stopping her*). Mariana, Lorenzo can find the man we need. (*As* MARIANA *pauses, he turns to* LO-RENZO.) My son, we need a prompter. Go into the town and search for one.

MARIANA. Bring back a man who can read, and not some ignorant fool.

LORENZO (*comes out on the platform, a large square piece of red velvet in his hands*). I have already spoken to Don Pancho's son, Ramón. The one who peddles silks and threads to all the women in the towns nearby. He can read, yes, and write, too.

MARIANA (*her eyes fixed on the velvet, and speaking in a strangled voice*). Lorenzo! Lorenzo, for what is that red velvet?

LORENZO (*innocently*). To cover the prompter's box, my mother, so that all the world shall know we give a play.

MARIANA (*stalking up to the platform*). Where did you get it? Where did you find that strip of goods? (ESTEBAN *frantically signals to* LORENZO *to keep quiet.*)

LORENZO (*looking curiously at his father*). What is it, sir? Why do you not speak out? I cannot read such wavings of the hands. (ESTEBAN *sinks down on one of the benches with a helpless gasp.*)

MARIANA (*swings on him*). So! It was you who gave it to him, eh? Well, search your brain for clever, useless answers. Where did you find the velvet?

ESTEBAN (*pleadingly*). Mariana, you have not worn that dress in many years. Not once have you worn it since our wedding day.

MARIANA (*slowly*). My dress. My beautiful red dress. The dress I wore when I first met the man I loved. (*Glares at him.*) From which part did you cut it?

LORENZO (*helpfully*). From the back. (*Turns around and makes an effort to show her how high up the cut came.*) You could replace the goods with a piece of red silk. Besides, when you are talking to your friends, they would not peer behind to see the difference.

MARIANA (*bursting into tears*). Oh, love of God and all the little angels! When was a woman so afflicted with such fools for a family?

ESTEBAN (*awkwardly patting her shoulder*). I know, my sweet, my heart's queen, my little cooing dove, that you have kept it out of sentiment. But you have other gowns that you first wore at our early meetings.

MARIANA (*jerking away from him*). I said I wore it when I met the man I loved, not the ass I married! (*Blazing out at them.*) Get out of my sight, the two of you! Oh, saints in Heaven, you and your plays and goats, and my red velvet gown. (*Her voice drops to a quiet deadly tone.*) I will make you pay for this, my friend. (*Girls' voices are heard in the street.*)

LORENZO (*excitedly*). We must draw the curtains. The audience arrives.

MARIANA. Will you leave before I break a piece of wood across your heads? (*Screams.*) Get out!

ESTEBAN (*jumps up on platform*). We had best leave, my son. Your mother feels a little nervous.
(*As they start out* ESTEBAN *looks at* MARIANA, *who has walked to the gate and has her back turned to them. He runs to the prompter's box, drapes it with the velvet, then hastily pulls the curtains as the girls appear at the gate. He and* LORENZO *disappear through the platform door.*)

MARIANA (*opening the gate*). Enter, enter. Our house is yours.
(ESTER, LOLA, *and* CARMEN *enter. Their skirts are of striped material, their blouses very white and clean. Their hair falls in two plaits over their shoulders, and they possess the wild, shy beauty of young deer. All three have on shawls. When they speak their voices are high and shrill and sweet, and they have the habit of giggling behind their hands.*)

ESTER. Here is our money, Doña Mariana.

LOLA. Will Lorenzo play a part?
(*All giggle at* LOLA'S *boldness.*)

MARIANA (*beaming on them*). He will indeed.

CARMEN. May we sit anywhere we like?

MARIANA (*nodding*). Wherever you may choose to sit, save in the rocking-chairs. They are for Doña Berta and Don Pepe.

(*The girls giggle as they find their places.* RAMON *comes to the gate.* RAMON *is very handsome and knows it. He wears a stiff straw hat, a bright pink shirt, a black tie, brown trousers, and shoes that are more orange than yellow, with button tops. His voice drips with personality.*)

RAMON. Is this the house of one Esteban Elizondo? Is this the house where there will be a play?

MARIANA (*gazing thoughtfully at him. To her, any new man is subject to conquest. It is perfectly harmless. She has never been unfaithful to* ESTEBAN. *She just likes to know that she could be if she wanted to*). So you are old Don Pancho's youngest son, Ramón.

RAMON (*makes her a low bow*). Your servant, señorita.

MARIANA (*smiling faintly*). I am Lorenzo's mother.

RAMON (*steps back*). Impossible! Why, you do not look so old as he. (*Lifts her hand.*) Allow me to press a kiss upon your hand from my dirty mouth.
(ESTEBAN, *sticking his head through the curtain, sees this gallant gesture and glares at them.*)

LOLA (*tittering*). Good evening, Don Esteban.

ESTEBAN (*grumpily*). You may not speak to me. I am not here. I am behind the curtain. (*Trying to show his authority.*) Mariana! Take his money and let him in.

MARIANA (*shrugs her shoulders*). He is the prompter.

ESTEBAN (*snapping at her*). Then he should be safely in his box, and you changing your gown. I will not have you roll the eye at every man who comes along.

RAMON. Would you be jealous of me, Don Esteban, and I only a poor peddler of women's goods?

ESTEBAN. I trust no man when Mariana rolls the eye. Lorenzo will stand at the gate.
(LORENZO *sticks his head through the curtains below* ESTEBAN'S.)

CARMEN. Good evening, Lorenzo.
(*The three girls giggle.*)

LORENZO. Good evening, Carmen, Lola—(*He gives a deep sigh for he is in love with* ESTER.)—Good evening, Ester.

ESTEBAN (*sharply*). You may not speak to them. Are they not the audience? Are you not on the stage? You must stand at the gate and take the money in your mother's place.

LORENZO. But I cannot stand at the gate and learn my part.

ESTEBAN (*yelling, since the poor man is irritated beyond endurance*). You should know your part! You will stand where I direct you. (*Gives him a push, and* LORENZO, *who is holding the curtains, swings out, falling off the platform, taking curtains and* ESTEBAN *with him. The girls scream and stand up on their bench.* MARIANA *and* RAMON *laugh.*)

ESTEBAN (*from below the mass of curtains*). Help us up!

LORENZO (*wailing*). Ay, father, you are sitting on my stomach.

MARIANA (*strolling over to the jerking heap of curtains*). Do I stay and take the money, my dear love?

ESTEBAN. You will change your gown.

RAMON. Here comes Don Pepe climbing up the hill. He will enjoy this drama. Not every hero can be wrapped in blankets.
(*A low murmur of voices from the road at the left can be heard growing louder and louder.*)

MARIANA. Speak quickly, my sweet turnip.

ESTEBAN (*frantically fighting with the curtains*). Help me up and you can own the goat.

MARIANA (*trying to hide her laughter*). Will you lend your hand, Ramón?

RAMON (*makes her a deep bow*). For you, dear lady, I would cage the sun in a crystal lamp, and borrow a star's five points to bind your hair.

LORENZO (*moaning*). Father, will you get off my stomach?

ESTEBAN (*as RAMON helps him up*). I will, when peddling fools remember how to act instead of speaking airy verses to the moon's left ear. (*Moving threateningly toward RAMON.*) As for you, my fine friend—

MARIANA (*hastily*). No time for speeches now. Aid Lorenzo with the curtain.

LOLA. May we help?

MARIANA. You may indeed, with Don Pepe at our gates. I will hold him off until the task is finished.

RAMON (*gallantly*). My arm, lady?

MARIANA (*takes it with a smile meant to infuriate* ESTEBAN). Thank you, Ramón.
(*They exit through the gate.* ESTEBAN *hangs over it gazing jealously after them.* LORENZO *is putting up the curtain.*)

ESTER (*watching* LORENZO). You are very strong.

LORENZO. In all the valley there is no man so strong as I.

LOLA (*helping* LORENZO *with the curtain*). So Ester said yesterday. (*She giggles.*)

ESTER (*snaps at her*). You have no right to repeat my words.

LORENZO (*forgetting the curtain, steps down from the platform in front of* ESTER). You spoke of me ... yesterday?

CARMEN (*helping* LOLA *with the curtain*). You are the constant subject of her speech.

ESTER. Who gave you leave to tell such tales of me? (*Flounces over and sits on bench.* LORENZO *follows her.*)

LORENZO (*softly*). Will you be at the plaza tonight?

ESTER (*turns her back on him*). I do not know.

LORENZO (*moving around to see her face, but she promptly turns her back again*). If you are there, will you walk around with me?

ESTER (*pleasantly shocked*). Alone?

LORENZO (*boldly*). Alone. Three times around.

ESTER (*gasping for breath*). But that would say to all the world that we two were engaged!

LORENZO (*sitting beside her*). My father soon will have enough to buy a goat, and then two goats, and then a herd. He will give me money to buy a wedding gown for you, and slippers—small white slippers. (*As the final tantalizing bit, since any beggar could have real flowers.*) And orange blossoms fashioned out of wax.

ESTER (*turning away her head*). Who can marry anyone without a house?

LORENZO. We will have a house with floors of soft blue tile. There will be a patio with white flowers growing in it. And, at night, when the moon is shining, there will be a light of pure green silver on your face. The locusts will hum their scratchy tunes, and the gray mockingbirds will wake and sing to us.

ESTER. What will they sing?

LORENZO. Of other lands they've seen beneath the moon. Of dusky jewels shining on white arms. Of fields of flowers sweet in bloom. Night-blooming jasmine, and the pale filigree of oleander. Of lilies, fragile as your hands, and blossoming thorn too sweet for any man to know its fragrance.

ESTER (*moves to another bench and stands looking down at it*). Is that all?

LORENZO (*following her*). Perhaps they will sing of mountains like purple ships against the soft pink evening sky ... of cities that are pearls on the golden breasts of distant valleys—

ESTER (*whispering*). Is that all?

LORENZO (*softly*). Perhaps they will sing of blue tiled floors, and you and me. (*Catches up her hand.*) Will you walk around the plaza, three times, alone?

ESTER (*facing him and once again the flirt*). With you?

LORENZO. With me.

ESTER. Tonight?

LORENZO (*steps closer to her*). Tonight.

ESTER (*draws back. She hears voices in the street*). There is Don Pepe.

LORENZO (*catching her wrist*). But will you come?

ESTER (*jerks away from him, then laughs up into his face*). Perhaps! (*Runs up to* LOLA *and* CARMEN *at the platform.*)

Lorenzo (*catches his breath, then flings back his head and begins to sing triumphantly*).

Allegretto (♩ = 84)

Shadow of our lord, St. Peter,
The river lures me,
The river lures me.
And thus your love
Would my poor love allure...
My love allure.

Esteban (*turning*). Stop your cackling. Behind the curtains with you, and you, señoritas, to your chairs. (*The girls giggle as they return to their bench.*)

Lorenzo (*as he passes Ester, whispers*). Tonight? (Ester *tosses her head at him.* Lorenzo *and* Esteban *disappear behind the curtains as* Don Pepe, *the mayor of The Three Marys enters with* Doña Berta *on his arm. She is a large impressive-looking woman, while he is a tiny spry little man. A crowd of men and women follow them. The men wear various colored bandannas knotted about their throats, and the white pyjama suits of the tropics, while the women are in colors as brilliant as the birds of the jungle country. They are all in a very gay humor, ready to enjoy the play.*)

Don Pepe (*impressively*). I have not seen a play upon the stage since I was last in the United States. (*He *leads* Doña Berta *to the rockers.*) Good evening, Carmen, Lola, Ester.

Lola. Do they have plays upon a stage in the United States?

Don Pepe. They have the photographs of people who walk across a screen and talk like you or me.

Carmen (*giggles*). Oh, Don Pepe, what a tease you are.

Don Pepe. And what is more, they can make their water hot or cold with merely the turning of a handle.

Man from Crowd. Now, Don Pepe, would you play with us?

Don Pepe (*with a luxurious sigh*). Ay, it is an education to travel.

Doña Berta. I prefer my own bed every night.

Ester. Is it true that girls can walk with men, even though they are not engaged?

Don Pepe. It is indeed.

Doña Berta (*scandalized*). A most immoral custom. Put not such foreign thoughts in our girls' heads, Don Pepe.

Don Pepe (*rises and makes her a low bow, then sits down again*). Always your obedient servant, Doña Berta.

Mariana (*to* Ramon). You had best get into the prompter's box, while I change my gown.

RAMON. If you need aid—

MARIANA (*tosses her head*). Then I will not call for you, my saucy lad. (*She goes into the bedroom right.*)

RAMON (*as he steps into the box the audience claps loudly. He holds up a modest hand*). I am but the prompter, my friends.

MAN FROM CROWD. Long life to the prompter. (*The audience claps loudly again. RAMON makes another bow, and lowers himself into the prompter's box.*)

LOLA (*whispers*). Ester, did Lorenzo ask you anything?

ESTER. Why should I tell you what was said?

CARMEN. We would keep your words as secret as a priest at confessional.

DOÑA BERTA. What would you keep secret, Miss?

CARMEN. Ester spoke with Lorenzo all alone.

DOÑA BERTA (*scandalized*). What?

DON PEPE (*startled*). Eh?

ESTER (*defensively*). Lola, Carmen, and Don Esteban were here.

LOLA. But just we three. That is almost the same as being alone.

DOÑA BERTA. That is your wild advice taking root, Don Pepe.

DON PEPE. Girls and boys must speak together. How else
would marriages arrange themselves?

DOÑA BERTA. When I was young, girls listened to their
parents.

MAN FROM CROWD. Is that why you have remained a
spinster, Doña Berta?
(*Loud laughter from the crowd.*)

DRUNK IN CROWD (*sings tune of* La Cucaracha).

　　　All the maidens are of gold
　　　And the married ones of silver.
　　　All the widows are of copper
　　　And the others merely lead.
　　　La cucaracha, la cucaracha...

DOÑA BERTA (*stands. She is furious*). Is this the gathering
place of drunks?

DON PEPE (*standing*). Take out the fool.

DRUNK. I paid my money—

DON PEPE (*in his most thundering voice*). What did you say?

DRUNK. I said . . . I need another drink. (*He staggers to the gate, then staggers back and shakes his finger at* DOÑA BERTA, *as he sings tauntingly*.) And the others are of lead . . .
(DON PEPE *signals to a man in the crowd, who drags the drunk outside the gate and then returns to his own bench*.)

DOÑA BERTA (*reseating herself*). Such common men deserve to stay in jail, Don Pepe.

DON PEPE (*flinging out his hands*). He stays in jail so much, Doña Berta, that he keeps his clothes there and calls it his hotel. I gave him the key to his cell yesterday. I became quite bored with locking it to keep him in, and then unlocking it to let him out.
(LORENZO *sticks his head through the curtains. There is loud applause from the audience*.)

LORENZO (*grinning and nodding his head, then to the prompter*). Ramón. (RAMON *sticks his head above the prompter's box*.) Can you perform on the harmonica?

RAMON. Alas, my only talent is for the drums.

LORENZO (*woefully*). But who will play the applause music?

MAN FROM CROWD. We will sing it for you.

LORENZO. Thank you, my friend. (*Steps in front of the curtain*.)

AUDIENCE (*sings lustily*).

> Now the duck is in the pot
> Bubbling for the fire is hot,
> Lifts his head and calls for savor,
> Add an onion for the flavor. (*They applaud loudly.*)

LORENZO (*bows and shakes his own hands over his head to the audience*). This is a tragedy of laughter, and a comedy of tears.

MAN IN CROWD. Long live the drama!
(*Shouting and applause from the crowd.*)

LORENZO. Its story I need not tell you, for you will see it for yourselves upon the stage. We ask you to laugh where laughter is needed, and for your tears where you should weep. If you go home contented, our labor has been repaid. (*Retires behind the curtain.*)
(*More shouts and applause from the audience.*)

MARIANA (*strolls in from the bedroom, dressed in a brilliant costume and with flowers in her hair*). I am the heroine. Will some kind gentleman aid me to the platform?

DON PEPE (*hastening to her*). May I be of service? (*Whispering as he lifts her to the platform.*) Was there enough to buy the goat?

MARIANA (*laughs*). Quite enough, my friend. Thank you. (*Disappears behind the curtain.*)

LOLA (*nervously tittering*). Oh, I am so excited.

CARMEN. Someone is pulling back the curtain.

(ESTEBAN, *a large straw hat on his head, a gaily-striped blanket over one shoulder, and carrying a gun, now pulls back the curtains. There is loud applause from the audience.*)

CROWD (*sings*).

Beans and corn and sweet potatoes,
Add a touch of red tomatoes.
Forget your sobs and your great sorrow,
We will all be drunk tomorrow.

(ESTEBAN *strikes an heroic attitude. There is a silence. Again he strikes an attitude. Again there is silence. He leans over and knocks on the prompter's box.*)

RAMON (*pops out his head*). Eh?

ESTEBAN (*impatiently*). Well . . . begin.

RAMON (*blankly*). Were you ready?

ESTEBAN (*takes a deep breath*). St. Peter give me patience! (*Thunders.*) We are ready!

RAMON (*lightly*). I have no book.

ESTEBAN. And you call yourself a prompter!

RAMON. No, a peddler. (*Seizing the opportunity, he stands and faces the audience*.) Ladies of the audience, I have silks and satins, wedding gowns and gowns for mourning, threads and pins to make you beautiful—

ESTEBAN (*screams*). Enough! (*More quietly*.) This is a noble drama, not a sale of women's clothes. (*Calling through the door*.) Lorenzo, the book.

LORENZO (*tosses the book through the curtains*). Here you are, father.

ESTEBAN (*hands it to* RAMON, *who sinks down into the box. Again* ESTEBAN *strikes an attitude*). Begin!
(*The prompter speaks rapidly in a clear, monotonous voice with the actors, but he is usually just a word ahead of them*.)

EST. AND RAMON. I am a soldier home from the war—

AUDIENCE. Bravo!

EST. AND RAMON. I am the bravest man in Mexico!

AUDIENCE. Long live the Republic! Long live Mexico!

EST. AND RAMON. I am returned after twenty years to see my wife and child.

MAN IN CROWD. The Revolution only lasted eight years.

ESTEBAN (*glaring at him*). Is this my war or yours?
(*Here* ESTEBAN *reads one speech and* RAMON *another*.)

RAMON. How I love my beautiful wife—

ESTEBAN. I am returned after thirty years—(*Bangs on prompter's box.*) You are ahead of me, Ramón.

RAMON. Did I know you were going to repeat? (*Reading.*) To see my wife and son.

ESTEBAN (*exasperated*). I have already said that.

RAMON. Well, say it again.

LORENZO (*sticking head through the door*). Father! (*Crooks a finger at him.*)

ESTEBAN (*walks to the door*). Well, what do you want?

LORENZO (*in a loud whisper*). You entered too soon. We are supposed to be ahead of you.

ESTEBAN (*who is rapidly losing his patience*). I wrote this play, and if I wish to be ahead of you, I will be first.

LORENZO. Mother says that if she does not enter now she will not act at all.

ESTEBAN (*who recognizes defeat when he sees it. He sighs*). Very well. (*Comes down to the edge of the platform and speaks to the audience.*) Pretend I have not been here. I will return in a little while. (*Goes through door to much applause from the audience.* MARIANA *and* LORENZO *enter.*)

MAR. AND RAMON. I fear your father soon returns from the distant wars.

LOR. AND RAMON. Father? You told me that he died long years before I was born.

Mar. and Ramon. There is a weight within my breast. I have always felt it there before I saw your father. (*Loud stamping noise behind platform door.*) I hear him now, the ghostly beat of horse's hoofs. (*Falls to her knees.*) Oh, Holy Virgin, save me from his wrath.

Lor. and Ramon. I will see who comes. (*He runs out through door.*)

Mar. and Ramon (*she beats her chest*). Ay, ay, ay.

Lor. and Ramon (Lorenzo *re-enters immediately, wearing a false mustache*). My wife!

Mar. and Ramon. My husband! (*They fall into each other's arms. She draws back.*) I may no longer call you husband.

Lor. and Ramon. What news is this? What sad words beat against my brain?

Mar. and Ramon. I fear Lorenzo's father does return today.

Lor. and Ramon. You told me he was dead.

Mar. and Ramon. And so I thought, but in the cards I read of a dark man, a dangerous man, and he is very dark, and very dangerous.

Lor. and Ramon. Your speech has stabbed me—

Lorenzo (*in a loud whisper to* Ramon). Speak louder, Ramón.

LOR. AND RAMON (RAMON *is laughing so hard his words are muffled*). My heart is rent in twain.

LORENZO (*to* RAMON). How can I hear you if you laugh, you fool?

LOR. AND RAMON (*both begin to shout, but* RAMON *wins*). I die, I die—I am dead! (LORENZO *stretches himself carefully out on the platform.*)

MAR. AND RAMON. Help, help, he is dead. (*She kneels beside him, lifts up her arms, then looks at the audience.*)

MARIANA. Silence, please. This is the sad speech.

MAR. AND RAMON. Oh, saints in Heaven, protect me from the wrath of man. Guard in your arms this poor sweet soul whose only sin—(*She gives a long sob.*)—was loving me too much.

ESTER (*wailing*). Oh, Carmen, Lorenzo is dead!

LORENZO (*sitting up*). I will return to life if you will walk around the plaza with me.

MARIANA (*pushes him down*). Lie down, you fool. You are dead. (*To* RAMON.) What happens next?

RAMON. You carry him out.

MARIANA (*in a loud whisper*). Lorenzo, this is where you go out. (LORENZO *stands*). Walk like a ghost. Remember, you are dead.
(LORENZO, *in as ghost-like a manner as possible, vanishes through the platform door.*)

Mar. and Ramon. I am a widow once again. Oh, Heaven. Oh, Saints. Oh, Love. (*She follows* Lorenzo *out.* Esteban *enters with his face turned to the side, proving that he cannot see* Mariana.)

Esteban (*to the audience*). You remember that I am home, so we will continue from where I was ... (*He glares at the platform door.*) ... interrupted. I am ready to begin, Ramón.

Est. and Ramon. I bear upon my chest the scars of war. (*Loud applause from the audience.*) Once I was wounded—(*Loud applause.* Esteban *holds up his hand.*)

Esteban. You are not supposed to clap there.

Est. and Ramon. Once I was wounded, but my enemy was cut to bits, and now I am home again to feast my eyes upon the beauty of my wife. (*Knocks on the door.*) Are all within here deaf?

Lorenzo (*without the mustache, enters*). Father! (*Falls to his knees.*)

Est. and Ramon (*draws back with dramatic surprise*). And who are you?

Lor. and Ramon. Your son.

Est. and Ramon. My son? Your age?

Lor. and Ramon. Nineteen.

Ester. Lorenzo! You told me you were twenty-two.

DON PEPE. This is a play, child, not a truth.

EST. AND RAMON (*with a glare for the interruption*). A son of mine nineteen, and I from home for thirty years?

MAN IN CROWD. You said twenty the first time.

ESTEBAN. Did I not write this play? If I choose to change the date then I change the date, with no advice from you!

EST. AND RAMON. Where hides the woman you call mother, and whom I once called wife!

ESTEBAN (*to the audience*). You can applaud for that. (*Loud applause.* ESTEBAN *modestly waving his hand.*) Thank you, my friends.

EST. AND RAMON. Where is she?
(MARIANA *enters.*)

MAR. AND RAMON. Ay, Federico!

EST. AND RAMON. Ysabela, my love—

MAR. AND RAMON. My husband! (*They embrace.*)

EST. AND RAMON (ESTEBAN *draws back from her*). One moment! Explain how it is that I have a son nineteen, and I from home ... (*He comes down and glares at the man in the crowd.*) ... forty years!

MAR. AND RAMON. I thought that you were dead, completely dead.

EST. AND RAMON. Kneel down.

MAR. AND RAMON (*she kneels*). I was young and beautiful, and weak to a man's whisper.

EST. AND RAMON. I must commune within my mind,
secret and alone.

ESTEBAN (*goes down and faces audience*). What shall I
do? What would you do, my friends?

MAN IN CROWD. Shoot her!

ANOTHER MAN. Chop off her head!

DOÑA BERTA (*in a trembling voice*). Forgive her.

ESTEBAN (*raps on prompter's box*). What do I do now?

RAMON. You choke her.

EST. AND RAMON (*he returns and begins to choke* MARI-
ANA). So shall all men deal with unfaithful wives.
(*Loud applause from the audience.* ESTEBAN *bows and
goes down to edge of platform, shaking his own hands
above his head.*)

AUDIENCE (*singing*).

> Hungry now the neighbor's look,
> Stand and wait and watch it cook.
> But alas, they must not eat it.
> Bravo! Bravo!!!

ESTEBAN. Thank you, my friends. (*Goes back and finishes choking* MARIANA. *She falls dead.*)

EST. AND RAMON. So am I revenged. (*He kicks her.*)

MARIANA (*sits up angrily*). That kick was not in the play!

ESTEBAN. Shh . . . lie down. You are dead.

MARIANA. Not too dead to deal with you, you ancient eater of cow's meat. (*Reaches out and grasps one of the vases on the prompter's box and throws it at him. He ducks, and it smashes on the floor. She screams.*) Ay, it was my own vase! I thought it was Doña Berta's.

DOÑA BERTA (*stands*). So I am not only insulted, but my property is destroyed as well. I stay no longer here! (*Sweeps out of the patio with hurt dignity.*) (*The audience rises.*)

ESTEBAN (*wringing his hands*). But the play is not finished. I have still a beautiful speech.

MARIANA (*jumps down from the platform*). Say it alone! I am finished with your drama. (*Runs into bedroom right.*)

RAMON (*climbs out of the prompter's box*). As for me, I prefer a good bottle of beer in the saloon. I have money, my friends. Who joins me?
(*With much cheering the audience, with the exception of* DON PEPE, LOLA, CARMEN, *and* ESTER, *press forward to shake* ESTEBAN's *hand, and then follow* RAMON *through the gate.*)

ESTEBAN (*sits down on the edge of the platform*). My beautiful play.

Don Pepe (*comfortingly*). It was an excellent drama, my friend. I think that we can arrange about the goat. (*To the girls.*) Shall I walk with these three pretty flowers?

Lola (*giggles*). Ay, Don Pepe.

Carmen. Will you tell us all about the United States?

Don Pepe (*beaming*). With the greatest of pleasure.

Lorenzo (*who has worked his way around to* Ester). Ester.

Ester (*earnestly*). When you died I knew the truth.

Lorenzo. Will you be on the plaza tonight?

Ester (*stamps her foot*). No.

Lorenzo (*crestfallen*). You ... won't?

Ester. Not unless you should be there, too. (*Runs out through the gate.*)

Lorenzo. Ester! (*Runs out after her.*)

Don Pepe. My three flowers have shrunk to two—one for each arm. (*He extends his crooked arms and the girls take them.*)

Lola (*as they exit through the gate*). Do they have such beautiful dramas in the United States?
(Esteban *sinks his chin in his hands and takes a long sniffling breath.* Mariana *enters, dressed in a bridal gown. She parades up and down in front of him.*)

ESTEBAN (*sighs*). The play is finished, but at least we have enough to buy the goat. (*Notices her for the first time.*) What are you wearing?

MARIANA. A bridal gown, which you could see if you were not so blind, my fool.

ESTEBAN. Have I seen that gown before?

MARIANA. I think not. It has only just been purchased. (*Preens herself.*)

ESTEBAN (*springing up*). From Ramón? (*He catches her wrist.*)

MARIANA (*pulling her hand away*). From the peddler of silks and satins, threads and pins, to make all ladies beautiful.

ESTEBAN (*narrowing his eyes*). With what did you pay for that gown?

MARIANA (*touching her dress lightly*). With the money that I took in at the door.

ESTEBAN (*squeaking*). The money for my goat?

MARIANA. No, my love. (*Jerks the velvet from the prompter's box and holds it out towards him.*) The money to replace an ancient gown of bright red velvet. (ESTEBAN *grasps his head and moans.*)

CURTAIN

THE UNITED STATES
(JEWISH)

WHEREFORE IS THIS NIGHT

BY *Violet Fidel*

THE CHARACTERS

As originally produced by The Carolina Playmakers on their One Hundred and Ninth Bill of Experimental Productions of New Plays in The Playmakers Theatre, Chapel Hill, North Carolina, April 18, 1946.

MRS. LEWISSOHN .... Marguerite Whitfield
MR. LEWISSOHN .... Max Paul
MRS. KATZ .... Gloria Day
JACK .... Sidney Shertzer
FLORENCE .... Maidie Davis
HARVEY .... Bill Sessions

THE SCENE: Newark, New Jersey. The dining room of the Lewissohn home.

THE TIME: The present. 6:00 o'clock on Passover eve.

THE SCENE

The curtain rises on a somewhat shabby dining-room of undistinguished taste, rather old-fashioned. The furniture looks as if it had been bought piece by piece at various times without much thought for style or harmony. Down right, near the footlights, is an old-fashioned armchair, and up left is a sideboard with some glass and china dishes on it. Prominently displayed near the center is the Passover table with five chairs around it. There is a door in the right wall leading to the kitchen, a window down left looking out onto the street, and a door at the left in the back opening into the hall. Hanging conspicuously on the rear wall is a plaque, such as is won by a student in school for an outstanding accomplishment. MRS. LEWISSOHN, *about forty-five, foreign-born, and* MRS. KATZ, *a neighbor, about thirty and brassy, come in from the kitchen.* MRS. KATZ *has a plate of haroset* [1] *in her hands.*

MRS. KATZ. So thanks again for the haroset, Mrs. Lewissohn.

MRS. LEWISSOHN. It's nothing. Nothing.

MRS. KATZ. Aw, it is. Even if I don't have time to make a real A-1 Passover Seder [2]—something a little fancy

---

1. Haroset is a mixture of nuts and apples, used in the Passover meal as a symbol of part of the flight out of Egypt.
2. Jewish festival held each year as a time of thanksgiving for the deliverance of the Children of Israel from bondage. It is a symbolical meal, usually attended by the whole family.

(*She indicates the table.*)—at least I'll have a couple of trimmings for Joey and the baby.

MRS. LEWISSOHN (*following* MRS. KATZ *to the hall door*). How's the baby feeling, Mrs. Katz?

MRS. KATZ. Better, knock wood, but I still have my hands full with him, I can tell you.

MRS. LEWISSOHN. With children you always have your hands full. I can tell *you.*

MRS. KATZ. Well, at least yours are grown already.

MRS. LEWISSOHN (*moving toward the table*). So what does that prove? Mrs. Katz, just because I got them safe out of rompers, do you think I stopped my worrying?

MRS. KATZ (*stepping back into the room*). What are you worrying about now—if your boy, Jack, is coming home tonight for the Seder? (*Pause.*) Mrs. Spector said she heard he wasn't coming.

MRS. LEWISSOHN (*annoyed*). Mrs. Spector knows? On Passover eve yet, he shouldn't come. (*She begins to arrange the table.*)

MRS. KATZ. Well, I'd sure like to meet him. You know, since I moved in here, that's all I been hearing about from the neighbors: "The Lewissohn's boy, Jack, is such a big-shot executive in New York." Everybody should have such a son.

MRS. LEWISSOHN (*looks up, embarrassed but pleased*). Yeah. Yeah.

MRS. KATZ. Do you think I'm kidding you, Mrs. Lewis-sohn? You can take my word. Everybody in the house who comes in to use my phone, so soon as we get to talking about what's doing, they tell me again about your Jack.

MRS. LEWISSOHN. I should maybe be embarrassed with such talk, but I'm not. When you got a son who's only twenty-six and already they're talking of him for a partner. (*Stops.*) Nu,[1] don't get me started, Mrs. Katz, or I'll never get my Passover table ready. (*She busies herself with the dishes once more.*)

MRS. KATZ. Such a table you set.

MRS. LEWISSOHN. Why not? My Jack sent the money for it. He knows it makes me happy. Yeah. He remembers —even away from home.

MRS. KATZ. Well, I'd better be going. (*Moving toward the door.*) Good-by, Mrs. Lewissohn. (*Calling back into the kitchen.*) Mr. Lewissohn—Florence. (*Then to Mrs. Lewissohn once more.*) And remember, I want to see this marvelous Jack a minute.

MRS. LEWISSOHN. I don't know if I want to give him up for even a minute—when he does come.

MRS. KATZ. But you're sure he's coming?

MRS. LEWISSOHN. Absolutely.
(MRS. KATZ *goes out, passing* HARVEY, *a boy of about fifteen. He closes the door noisily.*)

1. Yiddish expression, meaning "Well."

HARVEY. She thinks she's so much in this world. Just 'cause she owns a telephone.

MRS. LEWISSOHN. Such talk. Even if it's true. And you. A fine time to first come into the house.

HARVEY. I was out playing stickball with the gang. Till it began getting dark. (*He flings his hat onto the sideboard.*)

MRS. LEWISSOHN. On Passover eve yet.

HARVEY. Jack hasn't come.

MRS. LEWISSOHN. He's on his way.

HARVEY. The last train from Washington got in ten minutes ago. The last train before it's real dark.

MRS. LEWISSOHN. He was on it. I got a feeling.

HARVEY (*crossing to his mother*). Oh, Ma, Mrs. Hoffman across the hall said to tell you her Bennie called from the station. He and his wife are riding in from Philadelphia. They'll be there (*pointing across the hall*) in a while.

MRS. LEWISSOHN. And she was worried he wouldn't be here. I told her for Passover dinner all the children come home. Especially a good boy like her Ben. Don't worry, I said.

HARVEY (*going over to the armchair*). Yeah. He's a swell guy, Ben. Before he got married and moved, remember, he would take me to the ball games all the time.

MRS. LEWISSOHN (*derisively*). Ball games.

HARVEY (*sitting*). When I was little, so I couldn't go myself.

MRS. LEWISSOHN. Only if you thought a little less about baseball and more about your studies, your father would like it better.

HARVEY. Ah, Pa just don't understand baseball. Neither does Jack. (*Disgusted.*) He didn't even know the Yankee players.

MRS. LEWISSOHN. Oy, such a disgrace. (*Points to the plaque on the wall.*) When your brother, Jack, was even younger than you, he was out making good money like a man. This plaque he won for selling more magazines . . .

HARVEY (*he has heard this countless times*). I don't want to sell magazines. Can I help it?

MRS. LEWISSOHN. And such good marks he got in school, too. How he managed so much, I don't know. The burning ambition there is in that boy.

HARVEY (*gets up*). Hey—I hear steps. That's him.
(*They listen a minute.*)

MRS. LEWISSOHN. No. It's just Mrs. Katz going down the hall with a telephone message for someone. And telling the whole third floor Jack isn't here yet.
(HARVEY *goes over to the window and looks out. After a moment.*)

HARVEY. You can hardly see people passing by.

MRS. LEWISSOHN. Don't worry so much. He was on that train. Maybe he had to wait for a bus. Don't worry. (*She goes into the kitchen.*)

HARVEY. Who's worrying? I'm just getting hungry.

MRS. LEWISSOHN (*returning with two large spoons*). You should only not let your father hear you say that. (HARVEY *takes a piece of matzoth* [1] *from a dish on the sideboard.*)

MRS. LEWISSOHN. Is that Passover food you got there?

HARVEY. Don't kid, Ma. There's nothing else in this house. (*He sits down leisurely at table.*) Sure looks nice. Bet it's the nicest table in the house.
(MRS. LEWISSOHN *surveys the table with satisfaction.*)

MRS. LEWISSOHN. When you got a successful son to give it to you.

HARVEY. Gee, I'd like to see Jack again.

MRS. LEWISSOHN. He'll be here soon. So you can see him all you like.

HARVEY (*his voice becomes a little resentful*). All I like? When he does come, once in a pink moon, he runs in and out like a rabbit on wheels. Like Christmas week —when he stopped in between trains.

1. Unleavened bread. Leavened bread is forbidden during the holiday.

MRS. LEWISSOHN. So he's plenty busy.

HARVEY. You know, Ma, when I tell the kids in school I got a brother's a big engineering executive—that he has lunch with senators—and can get anybody's autograph —they think I'm kidding.

MRS. LEWISSOHN (*getting the dish of matzoth from the sideboard*). Kidding. Shmidding. Don't have to listen to what they say.

HARVEY. And when I show them the Cartwright and Caldwell stationery he bought once with his name, "John P. Lewis," written on it, they say—they say, "That's your brother? Prove it then."
(MR. LEWISSOHN, *fifty, foreign-born, dignified, enters from the kitchen on the last speech.*)

MR. LEWISSOHN. What're you talking? We got nothing to prove.

MRS. LEWISSOHN (*placing the matzoth on the table*). Still, it's nice people talk good about your kids, Sammie.

HARVEY. Pa, what does the "P." stand for in Jack's name?

MR. LEWISSOHN. It don't stand for nothing. It looks fancy on a big office door. Like "Lewis" looks fancy.

HARVEY. I think I'll let my name be Harvey S. Lewis.

MR. LEWISSOHN. You do first what your older brother did. Get yourself a real special scholarship. Get yourself a real special job.

MRS. LEWISSOHN (*pats the boy's head*). We'll be proud of Harvey, too, someday.

HARVEY. Me?

MRS. LEWISSOHN (*almost a prayer*). With our oldest son, God blessed us. With you and Florrie, too, things should turn out so good.

MR. LEWISSOHN. Harvey. Is he first in his class always, like Jack was? Even if he had to give up movies and baseball? No. He's last.

HARVEY (*getting up and going over to the stool down left*). Who wants to sit in and study? And I'm not *last*.

MR. LEWISSOHN (*taking a step toward* HARVEY, *earnestly*). You don't understand like Jack did. You ought to wanna get better marks than anyone. You ought to wanna be a credit to—

HARVEY (*sits*). I don't wanna get better marks. I'm smart enough.

MRS. LEWISSOHN (*pacifying them*). Such a way to argue on Passover night. (*She goes out to the kitchen.*)

MR. LEWISSOHN (*quietly*). Yeah. He's smart, Harvey. Too smart, sometimes.
(*He goes over to the window.*)

HARVEY (*teasing, restarting the argument*). I'm going to die of hunger in a minute. I wish I had a hot-dog—and mustard—and sauerkraut—on a nice crisp roll.

MR. LEWISSOHN (*turning toward him angrily*). I'll nice crisp roll you in the head. No bread comes into my house during Passover! In Jehovah's praise, we eat matzoth.

HARVEY. Tastes crummy. Boy, it sure is crummy.
(MR. LEWISSOHN *goes to the sideboard and picks up a large Bible.*)

MR. LEWISSOHN. Crummy. Crummy. All you can say?

HARVEY. What should I say then?
(MR. LEWISSOHN *seats himself at the table.* MRS. LEWISSOHN *comes back quietly from the kitchen and stands in the door.*)

MR. LEWISSOHN (*turns to Exodus*). "Then ye shall say it is the sacrifice of the Lord's Passover . . . who passed over the house of the children of Israel in Egypt . . ."

MRS. LEWISSOHN. Yeah. The Angel of Death passed over our houses.

MR. LEWISSOHN. ". . . when he smote the Egyptians and delivered our houses . . ."

MRS. LEWISSOHN. A funny kind of deliverance, sometimes I think.

MR. LEWISSOHN. ". . . and the people bowed the head and worshipped . . ."

HARVEY (*rises, respectful in spite of himself*). Gee, you must know that book by heart. You're always reading it.

MR. LEWISSOHN. So it's a bad thing to try to be a scholar? (HARVEY *moves over toward his father for a moment.*)

HARVEY. Nobody else's father I know of sits with his head in books. (*Goes to kitchen.*) Hey, Florence, you know where the macaroons are?

MRS. LEWISSOHN (*fondly looking after him*). Such a boy. A regular rascal.

MR. LEWISSOHN. He got no respect. Talks about bread like he would eat it.

MRS. LEWISSOHN. Listen, Sammie, our children got too much respect for such a thing. They were brought up right.

MR. LEWISSOHN (*sadly*). If taking the bread out of our mouths and stuffing it in theirs is right, yeah, they were brought up right. (*He rises.*)

MRS. LEWISSOHN (*genuinely questioning*). How else is there to bring up children?

MR. LEWISSOHN (*returning to the window*). I dunno, Pearlie. Who can say? Only ...

MRS. LEWISSOHN (*she follows him to the window*). Yeah?

MR. LEWISSOHN. You can only see shapes of buildings now—and all the windows are lit up.

MRS. LEWISSOHN. Like they started their Passover Seder already?

MR. LEWISSOHN (*slowly*). Yeah.

MRS. LEWISSOHN. Jack'll come.

MR. LEWISSOHN. The last train came in long time ago.

MRS. LEWISSOHN (*beginning to tire of making excuses*). I dunno, Sammie, maybe it was late.

MR. LEWISSOHN. Still, we gotta begin on time.

MRS. LEWISSOHN. So strict you are about it.

MR. LEWISSOHN. You call me "strict" yet? You've lived with me and all our people a whole life where there ain't so much that's ours. (*He goes to the table.*) Except our God and the memory of what we were. (*Taps on the Bible.*) So when it comes time to renew that memory again—maybe if we don't do it right . . .

MRS. LEWISSOHN. Yeah?

MR. LEWISSOHN. There'll be those who'll forget.

MRS. LEWISSOHN. Sammie, he didn't forget.

MR. LEWISSOHN. He ain't coming, Pearlie. What if I say that?

MRS. LEWISSOHN. You're as bad yet as the neighbors.

MR. LEWISSOHN. He ain't here.

MRS. LEWISSOHN. Like the boys in Harvey's class who don't believe the name on the stationery.

MR. LEWISSOHN. He ain't been here in a long time.

MRS. LEWISSOHN. You just don't understand, Sam, what a busy man your son is. The other week he flew to California. Then he flew back. The same day.

MR. LEWISSOHN. Tsk. Tsk.

MRS. LEWISSOHN. And it took Jehovah so many years to get the Jews out of bondage. Airplanes he should have used. Then he wouldn't have needed the Angel of Death.

MR. LEWISSOHN. You talk as bad as Harvey.

MRS. LEWISSOHN (*expanding as she talks about her son*). And just now he was in Washington—with Mr. Cartwright yet he went. He spoke to such big shots so close like I'm speaking to you, Sammie.

MR. LEWISSOHN (*grudgingly*). So, I'm proud of him, too.

MRS. LEWISSOHN. And he sent us a telegram he was there, didn't he?

MR. LEWISSOHN. Yeah. Always that boy sends telegrams. In the middle of the night we should think maybe he's hurt. We should only worry.

MRS. LEWISSOHN. Such a big man like he should take the time to write letters?

MR. LEWISSOHN. Once in a while, would it hurt? We took plenty time with him.

MRS. LEWISSOHN. So what else are parents supposed to do —but take time with children—(*She sits wearily.*) and then the children grow up. (*Her voice falls. For a minute, she, too, doubts.*)

MR. LEWISSOHN. And don't even come home on time for the Passover Seder.

MRS. LEWISSOHN (*with fresh vigor as if she were trying to convince herself*). He's a busy man, I say.

MR. LEWISSOHN. Yeah. I hear that and I hear that again. But does it answer my questions? Who are his friends? Does he still play at the piano? Does he ever go to the synagogue on Saturday?

MRS. LEWISSOHN. Yeah. I wonder, too. But should I be one of those mothers like Mrs. Hoffman who has to know what time her Ben brushes his teeth in the morning? And him a married man with a wife and kid in Philadelphia.

MR. LEWISSOHN (*sitting down opposite her*). Can't we ever find out about him? What his Mr. Cartwright is like?

MRS. LEWISSOHN. So Jack sent his picture he cut out from the financial page of the *New York Times*.

MR. LEWISSOHN. Yeah. Pictures he sends. (*His hands hit the table.*) But he don't come himself.

MRS. LEWISSOHN (*proudly*). Someday—you should find out—if your son becomes a partner.

MR. LEWISSOHN (*he has obviously thought of this before*). Will even that do me anything? He has this office in New York—across the bridge—and have any of us seen it? No. He never asked us.

MRS. LEWISSOHN. You expect him to sit in his office and entertain us yet?

MR. LEWISSOHN. No. I don't expect nothing from a boy who don't even come . . .
(HARVEY *and* FLORENCE *enter from the kitchen.*)

HARVEY. Still no Jack?

MRS. LEWISSOHN (*rising*). Patience, kind.[1]

FLORENCE (*crossing above the table to her mother*). Did he call from the station at Mrs. Katz's?
(MRS. LEWISSOHN *shakes her head.*)

HARVEY (*at the window*). You can't see anything anymore but street lamp shadows.
(FLORENCE *goes over to* HARVEY *and stands beside him.*)

FLORENCE (*at window*). And New York—a long ways off.
(*There is silence for a while.*)

MR. LEWISSOHN (*rising impatiently*). Are we going to stand at the window waiting all night? We gotta begin on time I say. Once a year when we do a thing, we do it right.

1. The Yiddish *kind*, child. Pronounced *kint*.

MRS. LEWISSOHN (*pleading*). Please, an extra minute at least we can give to Mr. Lewis of Cartwright, Cald-well—and Lewis.

MR. LEWISSOHN (*turning away*). So he isn't coming. (*After a moment he turns back to the finely-set table as if his mind were made up. MRS. LEWISSOHN takes MR. LEWISSOHN's arm as if to keep him back. Her voice is shrill.*)

MRS. LEWISSOHN. Do you ask me to sit down to my Pass-over dinner without my first-born son, Sammie? How can I eat what I cooked? It's turned to bitter herbs. How can I sit at the table and see his silverware, his dishes, and not him?

MR. LEWISSOHN (*turning his back on her*). Don't you think it breaks my heart, too, Pearlie, he shouldn't come?

MRS. LEWISSOHN (*the shrillness is gone. There is only softness, sympathy, as she describes her mother and herself*). My mother's first-born weighed thirteen pounds, she said. He came to America and died of smallpox. And she cried her eyes red in the old country. But who wouldn't cry for a first-born?

HARVEY. Hey, Pa. Florence says she's supposed to ask the Four Questions tonight. And I wanna say them. (*MR. LEWISSOHN sits above the table. HARVEY takes the chair at his right, MRS. LEWISSOHN at his left. FLORENCE is at the right of the table.*)

FLORENCE. Well, I'm the youngest.

HARVEY. But you're a girl. So you don't count.

FLORENCE. I know 'em real good.

HARVEY (*obviously the religion, this particular phase of it, appeals to him*). Girls never count. When we go to the synagogue even, the boys sit 'way down stairs where everyone can see them. And they hide the girls in the back.

FLORENCE. Ah—don't be mean. I wanna ask the Questions. I know 'em: "Wherefore is this night of Passover so different from all other nights in the year?"

HARVEY. Yap. Yap. Yap.

FLORENCE (*proud of her religion. And herself*). "... in the year." He's just trying to make me forget, but he can't do it. I know it so good ... "On all other nights we eat either leavened or unleavened bread. Why on this night do we eat only matzoth which is unleavened bread? On all other nights ..."

HARVEY (*teasing* FLORENCE). Sharp as matzoth and twice as crummy.

MR. LEWISSOHN. Shh. Such a racket the neighbors have to hear on a night when we should be quietly thanking God. (Pause.) *All* of us.

MRS. LEWISSOHN. If you were worrying about the neighbors, Sam, you'd wait till he came.

FLORENCE (*eagerly*). Who's going to ask the Four Questions?

MR. LEWISSOHN (*after a moment's hesitation, he decides*). You, Florence.

HARVEY. But, Pa—

MR. LEWISSOHN. You have a bigger part tonight, Harvey. You sit on the right of your father.

MRS. LEWISSOHN (*her last effort failing*). Wait a little only.

MR. LEWISSOHN. My faith is important to me. As it was important to my fathers. And should be to my sons. Put the wine out, Pearlie.
(*They are all seated. MRS. LEWISSOHN pours out the wine. The men put on skull caps. The ceremony begins.*)

MR. LEWISSOHN. "Boroch atto Adenoi Ellojanuh meloch h'olem boree pree haguffen . . ."
(*There is a knock on the door.*)

MRS. LEWISSOHN (*rising quickly and going to door*). It's Jack! See. I said we should have waited. Ach, such a boy yet!

FLORENCE. I heard Mrs. Spector say he wouldn't come.

MRS. LEWISSOHN (*at open door*). Jack, mein kind.
(*JACK enters. He is a very fine-looking boy of twenty-six, dressed expensively and well. At the present moment, dishevelled, he looks tired. He is carrying a large paper bag. It is not immediately obvious, but soon becomes so, that JACK is drunk.*)

JACK (*a forced impersonality in his tone*). Ma.
(*He pushes her away as she starts to embrace him.*)

FLORENCE. Pa didn't think you was coming.

HARVEY (*rising and going to* JACK). So he started in
without you.

MR. LEWISSOHN. I was hoping you'd be here early ...
like it mattered.
(*He remains seated.* FLORENCE *rises and follows* HAR-
VEY *over to* JACK.)

FLORENCE. What you got there?

JACK (*advancing ahead of them into the room, left of the
table*). Easy now. I'm not Santa Claus. (*The symbols
of the outside world come easily to him.*)

MRS. LEWISSOHN. Were you on the last train from Washington, kind?

JACK (*trying to be casual*). Trains? Who bothers with
trains?

HARVEY (*awed*). Did you *fly?*

JACK. L. A. and I drove up from Washington in my new
car—nice job.

HARVEY. You got a new car?

JACK (*too proudly*). Naturally. All us big shots have
cars. Hot off the assembly line.

HARVEY (*following closely behind* JACK). What color is it?

JACK (*vaguely*). Red. With a gray dashboard.

FLORENCE. Gee whizz!

HARVEY. Can we ride in it?

FLORENCE. Can we see it? Is it out in front of the house?

JACK. No. L. A. took it. He dropped me off here and drove downtown to get some golf balls.

HARVEY. Golf? Can you play golf?

JACK (*unbuttoning his overcoat*). Sure. We're going to play this week end. I play golf. I play tennis and I play gin rummy, too. I dance extremely well—drink like a gentleman—(*Still wearing his overcoat, he sits on the stool by the window.*)

MRS. LEWISSOHN (*a little worried*). Have you been drinking now, Jack?

JACK (*disregarding her*). Am polite and courteous at all times. I am a model young man in general.

MR. LEWISSOHN (*rising at table*). We always were proud of you, Jack.

JACK. L. A.'s proud of me, too. Putting me up for the Raquet Club this week end. It's right near his home on Long Island where we're going.

MR. LEWISSOHN (*coming down around the right of the table*). What is this Raquet Club, Jack?

JACK (*rises*). Oh, it's very exclusive. Very exclusive. (*He turns away from his father.*) Keeps all the undesirables out. They wear the right clothes and drink—and play at being sportsmen—

MR. LEWISSOHN (*patting* JACK, *he goes up to the sideboard*). Such foolishness we are talking about.

JACK. And L. A.'s putting me up for it this week end. (*He moves across the room.*) Johnny Lewis. Good guy, Johnny Lewis ... good ... (*He babbles on.*)

MR. LEWISSOHN (*getting out a skullcap from sideboard*). We'll talk yet later. We got a lot to talk about. But now we should go back to the Seder. (*He walks slowly down right to* JACK, *holding out one of the skullcaps.*) Jack, my first-born, since you come, I been yelling at you. Yeah. I dunno. It's just I'm so glad to see you. (JACK *laughs heartily, loud, finally almost hysterically.*)

MRS. LEWISSOHN (*disturbed*). Kind ...
(HARVEY *and* FLORENCE *stand near the window, silent, a little frightened.*)

MR. LEWISSOHN (*angrily*). Why do you laugh when I give you a yamelke? [1] Such a business.

JACK (*pulling off his overcoat*). Good fellow ... Johnny Lewis ... smart fellow ... knew this would happen too. (*He sinks in the armchair.*)

1. Skullcap.

MRS. LEWISSOHN (*moving toward him*). There are tears in your eyes.

JACK. Because I'm laughing so hard.

MRS. LEWISSOHN (*appealingly*). Yankel—Yankel—

JACK (*leaping up*). For God's sake, don't call me by that Jew name. I never liked it.

MR. LEWISSOHN (*thunders at him*). For God's sake were you named it!

JACK. I don't want a sermon. I didn't come for that.

MRS. LEWISSOHN (*sure of herself now*). He came because I wanted him. And he loves me, Sammie. (*She steps between* JACK *and* MR. LEWISSOHN.)

MR. LEWISSOHN. He came for the Seder. And he speaks so.

JACK. Sure. Now listen. (*He turns finally, and faces both his parents.*) I came because L. A. said: "Johnny, let's stop in Newark. I wanna meet your folks." I tried to tell him it was a crazy idea. I knew what'd happen. But he was tight—and anyhow—my old friend L. A.—(*His voice drops off sulkily.*)

MRS. LEWISSOHN. See, Sam, you was worried he didn't think of us. (JACK *walks away toward the back of the room with his head down.*)

JACK. Sure. I've told him lots. Yeah. Lots.

HARVEY. What did you tell him?
(JACK *lifts his head and walks around the table, between his parents, and* HARVEY *and* FLORENCE.)

JACK (*slowly, as if the memory were amusing to him*). What a big boy you are for your age. How you're getting such good marks in school.

HARVEY (*wryly*). Better marks than anyone.

JACK (*turning toward his sister*). And Florence—how she looked like her grandmother.

MRS. LEWISSOHN (*wondering*). What is this? You never seen her grandmother. She died of a broken heart in the old country.

JACK (*going on. His voice getting bitter*). And Mother and Dad. Yeah, I told him lots. All I remembered from the Andy Hardy pictures—I didn't see too many of them, though—and the Sunday supplement I rolled into Home, Sweet Home—Newark version.
(*He sinks down, uneasily, on the stool.*)

MR. LEWISSOHN. Do you have to make riddles now?

JACK (*staring straight ahead*). Riddles? Okay, I'll answer them. If I know any of the answers. I can't tell any more. You think you know. You're so damn sure you do. Then all of a sudden it slips away.

MRS. LEWISSOHN. So he's coming here—your L. A. Cartwright? After the Seder.

JACK (*sharply*). For supper.

Mrs. Lewissohn (*shocked*). But on Passover? Didn't you explain to him that he was an outsider? And no outsider—

Jack (*rising*). I don't have anything to explain to him. I'm real palsy with him. When he wants to come here, he can come.

Mrs. Lewissohn. If he's a friend of yours...

Jack. More like a father. He treats me like a son.

Mr. Lewissohn (*scornfully*). So *he* knows how to treat you like a son.
(Mrs. Lewissohn *shoos the children out of the room. This is nothing for them to hear.*)

Jack. Or a son-in-law. (Jack's *parents stare at him in silence.*) His daughter's real pretty—Julie—she's kind of little and young-looking. She's not so young—out of Wellesley four years. I mean she just looks... (*He crosses slowly, blindly, down right.*)

Mrs. Lewissohn (*softly, full of meaning*). Julie Cartwright—

Jack (*his tone changing, like a phonograph record*). Jews always prey on blonde Christian girls—like Julie. Fat, greasy Jews, with big dark hands. (*He holds his own hands up and examines them dazedly, turning toward* Mr. *and* Mrs. Lewissohn.)

Mr. Lewissohn. Jack!

Jack. Oh, I'm not saying it. Alex Hale said it—in the office the other day—that Goebbels said it... (*He *turns toward the armchair.*) Lotsa people. (*Sighs.*) I guess I been drinking.

MRS. LEWISSOHN. Too much, kind.

JACK. No. L. A. and I stopped in for a couple short ones —that's all. (*After a moment he turns angrily.*) Oh, you don't like that either. A good little Jew boy doesn't drink! Lips that touch liquor aren't supposed to kiss the hem of God's garments, huh?

MRS. LEWISSOHN (*looking toward* MR. LEWISSOHN, *worried*). Schweig still—your father—

MR. LEWISSOHN. Never mind his father, Pearlie. Worry a little about his forefathers. (*He moves past her toward* JACK.)

JACK (*going up to the left of the table and lifting a cup*). Nothing but sacrificial wine. Well, I'm tired of sacrifices. And I'm tired of a God who's forgotten His chosen people!

MR. LEWISSOHN. So we have not forgotten Him. (*He indicates that they proceed with the Seder.*)

JACK (*trying to make them understand*). Look, L. A.'s coming here soon. You think he's going to have Passover with us. Do you think the moon's made of pale green cheese, and God in His heaven gives a damn for us?

MR. LEWISSOHN (*stubbornly going to his seat at the table*). I am sitting down to my Seder.

JACK (*frantically going to the sideboard and getting the paper bag*). It's a good thing the A & P was open. Hooray for the Super Market and the great American dollar! This stuff won't take long to fix. And could you take the candlesticks off the table?
(*He pours the contents onto the table. Among them is a loaf of bread.*)

MR. LEWISSOHN (*stunned*). You brought a loaf of bread into the house yet?

JACK (*trying to be calm*). He'll expect bread.

MRS. LEWISSOHN. On Passover?

MR. LEWISSOHN. Jack! This profane food! Your profane friends! How can anyone who calls himself a Jew—?

JACK (*angrily*). I don't call myself a Jew.
(*Silence.*)

MRS. LEWISSOHN (*slowly crossing to him*). So they don't know.

JACK. And no one's going to call me one—if I can help it. Or the A & P can help it. Or any instrument of Heaven or Hell!

MRS. LEWISSOHN (*she is almost to him, but she stops short*). You're not going to tell them?

JACK. After I sweated blood that they shouldn't find out?

MR. LEWISSOHN. Because you're a coward.

JACK (*shaking his head*). Because I want to keep my job.

MRS. LEWISSOHN. But how *could* they fire you?

JACK (*advancing a little down left, but facing them now*). How could they? That's the question. How could they tell a man they don't want him in a job—they don't want him in a college? They don't want him anywhere they can see him—touch him—or—I dunno how they could. But they do, don't they?

MRS. LEWISSOHN (*appealingly*). But, Jack. Always you were so brilliant. Your professors said they knew—

JACK. Yeah. They knew everything but what you could read in a three-cent paper. I'm not any more brilliant than Alex Hale or Reed Corley, or a thousand other guys who want my job. And could get it—too damn easily.

MR. LEWISSOHN. Not so easily. If you worked harder than them.

JACK. Look. I'm tired of sitting in my room and studying. Of knowing more than anybody. I don't know anything but a ringing in my ears and an empty feeling in my stomach.

MR. LEWISSOHN. You're drunk. That's why.

JACK. And what did I get for a reward? They shook their heads and said, "Smart little Hebe," and slammed the door to their lives in my face.

MRS. LEWISSOHN (*she edges him toward the chair*). Kind, kind. You're tired.

JACK (*sitting down*). Yeah. I'm tired. Why do I always have to do more and get less?

MRS. LEWISSOHN (*sitting beside him*). I dunno, kind. Maybe—

MR. LEWISSOHN. Because we don't belong anywhere but at our Seder table. And that's God's truth.

JACK (*rising quickly*). Well, I want to belong. I want to join the Raquet Club and work for Cartwright and Caldwell—and visit L. A. on Long Island.

MR. LEWISSOHN. Such little things yet he worries about.

MRS. LEWISSOHN. No. They're big things, Sammie. Big heavy stones we wear around our hearts. Stones from which we build our Wailing Wall.

MR. LEWISSOHN. So if we don't want what God don't think we should have, we ain't got nothing to moan about.

JACK (*remembering the boy he was*). When I was in college, Ma, first I had my desk near the window, but I'd find I was looking out when I studied. I'd find myself watching the birds flying by and the boys playing tennis. I'd find myself relaxing. Yeah. Wasn't that awful? So then I moved my desk to where it faced the wall. (*His voice rises.*)

MRS. LEWISSOHN. Shhh, kind, the neighbors'll hear you.

JACK. I went all through college getting brilliant marks— just like that—the wall and I. But when I got out of college, I decided to climb over the wall.

Mr. Lewissohn. Plenty have tried it. It don't work.

Jack (*turning toward him*). Well, it worked with me. I'm Johnny Lewis of Cartwright and Caldwell with a shiny office and a swivel chair. (*Pause. His voice changes.*) What they say about the Jews—oh, I hear it —yeah. But I hear what they say about the price of eggs in Timbucktu. It doesn't affect me. It doesn't make me all tense and hurt inside. I just turn around in my swivel chair so they can't see my face.

Mrs. Lewissohn. Are you happy like this?

Jack. I don't know yet. But I want time to find out! That's all I want—time.

Mrs. Lewissohn. So. He'll respect us.

Jack. No. It doesn't work that way. It should, but I dunno, it doesn't. It'll be something out of his life and he won't bother to understand. Not that he's intolerant. He's not. He's a swell guy. Real good friend. Do anything for old Johnny Lewis.

Mr. Lewissohn (*bitterly*). Johnny Lewis.

Jack (*stepping between his mother and father*). All I ask is time. You've always given me so much. Now...

Mr. Lewissohn. Nu, maybe we gave you too much already.

Mrs. Lewissohn. On Passover, kind, you should only stay with us.

MR. LEWISSOHN. On Passover, yet, we rejoice for our first-born's salvation.

MRS. LEWISSOHN (*a note of determination in her voice. She pronounces the new name slowly, looking at* JACK *hard*). And you are my first-born—Johnny Lewis.

MR. LEWISSOHN (*incredulously*). What are you saying?

MRS. LEWISSOHN. I will make for him and his Mr. Cartwright something to eat. Is it too much to ask? Florrie, you and Harvey carry the Passover things to the kitchen.
(*The children, who have edged to the door, now enter eager, but bewildered, and start to do as they are told.* MRS. LEWISSOHN *is all activity.*)

MR. LEWISSOHN (*he realizes he is completely alone*). Yes, Pearlie. It is too much to ask. (*He stands very still.*)

MRS. LEWISSOHN (*stopping her work*). Does it matter where we have our Passover meal—or when, just so long as we thank God for delivering us from bondage? (*She realizes the grim humor of her words.*)

MR. LEWISSOHN (*moving toward her*). And you are sending us back into bondage.

MRS. LEWISSOHN (*firmly*). To set free my oldest son.

MR. LEWISSOHN. You are making a ghetto from the kitchen yet.

MRS. LEWISSOHN. So it'll be hard the neighbors should know we're not using such a Passover table like we had. But it doesn't matter—

MR. LEWISSOHN. So it'll be harder the neighbors should know we have such a son who—
(*There is a knock on the door.*)

JACK (*starting*). He's here. Oh, God.

MR. LEWISSOHN. You mention God. You've given up your God. You've traded Him in for a red car with a gray dashboard.

MRS. LEWISSOHN. Florence, open the door. And please, Sammie, don't speak much. You and me, we don't speak English so good—yeah?

MR. LEWISSOHN (*he turns away from the door*). So ashamed I am inside. How could I speak?
(FLORENCE *opens the door.* MRS. KATZ *enters.*)

MRS. LEWISSOHN. Mrs. Katz. Oh, it's you. Gott sei danken.
(*All stare as* MRS. KATZ *comes into the room.*)

MRS. KATZ. Yeah. It's me—with a telephone message for your boy, Jack. Is this Jack? I've heard so much about you. He's the image of his father.

JACK (*going toward her*). What's the message?

MRS. KATZ (*taking out a piece of paper*). Here. I wrote it down. "Meet L. A. Cartwright at the Clinton Bar. Immediately."

JACK. The Clinton Bar.

MRS. KATZ (*prying*). Yeah. I think that's what he said. He sounded kind of like he'd been drinking. Then he hung up. Is your job interesting?

JACK (*looking at the note*). Immediately.

MRS. KATZ. Yeah. Were you in Washington?

JACK. Uh-huh.

MRS. KATZ. I'd kind of like to go there. They didn't know if you was coming home for Passover. Isn't that a laugh? You started dinner, Mrs. Lewissohn?

MRS. LEWISSOHN (*impatiently*). Soon. Soon.

MRS. KATZ. Well, I'd better be going.

JACK (*he gets his coat from the armchair*). I'd better be going too.

MRS. KATZ (*interested*). Oh—(*she exits hurriedly.*)

MRS. LEWISSOHN. Was it necessary you should say that before Mrs. Katz?

JACK (*going toward table*). L. A.'s waiting.

MR. LEWISSOHN. L. A.'s waiting. So you must go running yet. Just like a monkey on a string—whose coat has some shiny brass buttons.

MRS. LEWISSOHN (*wistfully*). You cannot stay here with us? Not even for Passover?

JACK (*the forced impersonality that he came in with returns to his voice. More so than ever*). I didn't come home for Passover.

Mrs. Lewissohn. Nu, you will be getting hungry before you reach Long Island.

Jack (*he is gathering the packages into his paper bag*). Oh, I'll grab a sandwich and a couple drinks at the Clinton.

Mr. Lewissohn. You shouldn't drink so much.

Jack. Do you have to start that again?

Mrs. Lewissohn. Your father means it isn't good to drink when you got so far to drive.

Mr. Lewissohn (*tensely*). Much more than that I mean. But what can I say, Jack?

Jack. Don't worry. I drove up here pretty tight, and made it okay. Had a couple scrapes. But I made it okay. L. A. says I'm a damn good driver.

Mrs. Lewissohn (*putting her arms around him*). Take care, kind. Not fast. Not fast.

Jack (*brushing her away*). Sure. Don't worry. (*He goes toward the door, paper bag in hand.*)

Mrs. Lewissohn. Be always careful when you drive to-night.

Jack. Sure, Ma. So long. (*He weaves out, leaving the door open. They start going back to the table.*)

Mrs. Lewissohn (*looking out toward the hall*). I hope he knows not to make too much noise in the hall—so the whole house yet hears.

HARVEY (*more quietly than usual*). Gee, it's so late.
(*They all resume their former places at the table, standing.*)

MR. LEWISSOHN. Time is as nothing to the children of Israel. They wait, and yet they wait.
(*They sit. He begins the Boroch Atto in a low voice. From across the hall comes laughter and the sound of* MRS. HOFFMAN'S *voice.*)

MRS. HOFFMAN (*across the hall*). So, Bennie. How are you and Estelle? I was worried yet you wouldn't come. No son should—
(MRS. LEWISSOHN *rises and closes the door.* FLORENCE *begins the Four Questions.*)

FLORENCE (*haltingly, softly*). "Wherefore is this night of Passover so—so—different from any—all other nights—." I guess I don't remember it so good—. "On all other—nights—we—." Gee, Harvey—you can say 'em if you want to—

HARVEY (*soberly*). Yeah. "Wherefore is this night of Passover so different from all other nights—."

CURTAIN

UNITED STATES
(NEGRO)

WASHED IN DE BLOOD
A Negro Ritualistic Drama of Rural Georgia

BY *Rietta Bailey*

THE CHARACTERS

*As originally produced by The Carolina Playmakers
on their Fifty-second Bill of Experimental Productions
of New Plays in The Playmakers Theatre, Chapel Hill,
North Carolina, December 9, 1937. First published in*
THE CAROLINA PLAY-BOOK *for March, 1938.*

AUNT ANGELINE DEAN,
    a conjure woman .... Marguerite Lipscomb
LIZE NELSON,
    President of "The Knights of Moses" ...Lois Latham
SAPPORY NELSON, *Lize's daughter* Dorothy Browning
LOVIN' SAM .... Burr Leach

BILL,	⎫	⎧ John Morgan
Sappory's husband		
BOOTCHIE NELSON		Madeline Haynsworth
MOSE		Holman Milhous
RALINA	⎬ *sinners* ⎨	Virginia Kibler
JOSHUA		Tom Fearing
COOT NAN		Rose Peagler
LINSON		Jack Taylor
* PEARLY		Mary Louise Greene
* PRECIOUS MAE	⎭	⎩ Bolling Brown

PREACHER .... John T. Roughton
MEMBERS OF "THE KNIGHTS OF MOSES," *a burial society:*
    Jane Hunter, Frances Roughton, Virginia Giddens,
    Blanche Bullock, Rebecca Jordan, Margaret Jordan,
    Emy Hertz, Eugene Langston, Kalman Sherman.
    THE SCENE: A clearing in the piney woods near Mount
Zion Church, in Middle Georgia.
    THE TIME: The present. A spring night.

    * *These two characters are omitted from the printed version
of the play.*

THE SCENE

Going south from Macon, Georgia, deep into the woods, there is a narrow wagon road leading down a hill. It is damp and dark at the foot of that hill even when the moon shines through the pines. Long, gray moss, hanging soft from the giant oaks, makes a ghostly curtain in the darkness. It is said that spirits walk there in the night and moan when the moon is on the wane. The screech owls answer with a wailing sound and the wood creatures mumble low.

It is past midnight, dark and still. Deep shadows from the pines lie heavy, obscuring the road leading up the hill and Mount Zion Church, which stands on its crest. Seeping through the darkness, the moonlight falls on an old oak tree at the foot of the hill. The moss, hanging from its branches, touches the ground. Nearby, on a slow fire, rests a round, black pot.

This is the hour and the place for spirits.

Coming down to that brewing pot is the Negro conjure woman, AUNT ANGELINE DEAN. *She has been on this earth so long that she has forgotten the number of her years. Still the Lord sees fit to leave her here to help "carry on His Glory."*

AUNT ANGELINE *was born with the caul* [1] *on her face, and the power to conjure is strong in her. All the colored folks of the neighborhood fear and respect her. She cures them of the fevers and the love troubles. She hides them*

---

1. A sac sometimes covering a child's head at birth. Believed by primitive peoples to be a sign of prophetic powers.

*from the white man's law. She can feel out sin anywhere
in the county, and she catches up the sinners before they
fall too low. She has never been wrong in her prophecy
of the future, or failed to bring a sinner to repentance.*

AUNT ANGELINE *is small and bent with the misery.*[1]
She wears a white head-rag,[2] *a long gray dress, and a
white apron. Leaning on her crooked stick, she hobbles
slowly from behind the great oak and goes to the pot,
mumbling to herself as she walks. She is at home here in
the darkness. Her powers of conjure are brewing in that
pot. She stirs the brew with her stick, chanting slowly.*

ANGELINE.
> Round an' roun' I stirs de pot,
> Keeps de brew a-bubblin' hot.

(LIZE NELSON, *coming in from down right, interrupts
the chant. She is middle-aged, big, and fat. A Christian
and an exhorter, as President of* THE KNIGHTS OF
MOSES *she works with* AUNT ANGELINE *in the battle
against sin.* LIZE *comes quickly through the woods.
She looks about her frantically. Seeing* AUNT ANGE-
LINE, *she rushes toward her.*)

LIZE. Aunt Angie! Aunt Angeline!

ANGELINE (*paying no attention*).
> Juice ob de jimpsum, seed ob de pine,
> Snail and crawdad,[3] frog-legs nine.

LIZE. Aunt Angie, raise up here. Dis Lize.

1. Pain, usually rheumatism.
2. A kerchief.
3. Crayfish.

ANGELINE (*calmly*). Evenin', Lize.

LIZE (*hesitating to come near the brew*). Auntie, dat pot ain'—

ANGELINE (*interrupting*). Speak yo' min', Lize.

LIZE. Aunt Angie, you gots to come quick. Trouble settin' in my house, gwine bust loose 'fo' day.

ANGELINE (*unconcerned*). Yeah, I knows.

LIZE. Aunt Angie, it's Bill and Sappory. Bill settin' dere waitin' fo' her. He mad enough to kill. Auntie, give me a charm fo' de husband fits.[1]
(ANGELINE *does not answer.*)

LIZE. Aunt Angie, I done tromped t'r'u' dese dark woods ha'f de night, lookin' fo' you, an' callin' yo' name. You gots to come, Auntie.

ANGELINE. Dey ain' no work fo' me dere, dis night. De spirits am walkin' in de woods.

LIZE. Can't you visit Bill wid a scarin' sperit, Auntie? Sappory comin' in on dat 'scursion train. Dey ain't much time to ca'm Bill down. (*Pausing when* ANGELINE *does not reply.*) You gots to. Sappory my onlies' chile, Auntie.

ANGELINE (*beginning to take an interest*). On de 'scursion train?

1. A jealous temper.

LIZE. Yes'm, she went to Macon on de up-train, wid de balance ob de young folks. Dey comin' in on de down-train. Bill settin' dere waitin' fo' de whistle to blow. Visit him wid a sperit, Auntie. Git him ca'med down fo' dey come.

ANGELINE. I gits 'em all ca'med down, de sinners. Ain' I tole 'em, de triflin' niggers, a-cavortin' in town on a Sa'd'y?

LIZE. Dey ain't wile, Auntie, dey just pleasure deyself.

ANGELINE. Gits so pleasured dey cain't set in de Lawd's house on Sunday. Sappory's de wo'st one.

LIZE. Jedus, Auntie, she ain' did no harm.

ANGELINE (*looking into her pot*). I read out de trouble dey gettin' in, wid de debil a-leadin' 'em on. Dey marches down to de house ob sin where de drink am poured and de dice am roll'. Sappory took up wid a bright-skin man, a high-steppin' sinner wid a loose-tongue mouf.

LIZE. Oh, Lawd, de trouble fall!

ANGELINE. Yeah, dey sing an' strut. Dey cavort all night. Dey done fell from de grace ob de Lawd.

LIZE. Auntie, ain't you gwine sabe 'em? Dey jist baby lambs a-wanderin' from de fol'.

ANGELINE. I sabes 'em. I works de Plat Eye [1] wid a pow-erful han'.

1. A spell cast upon a sinner which makes him believe an eye watches his every act—evidently the eye of conscience.

LIZE (*terrified*). De Plat Eye! Do Jedus, Auntie! You say you would, but you ain' never brung de Plat Eye.

ANGELINE. De time hab' come an' de sperits am walkin'. De Plat Eye all dat can sabe 'em. Go git de Knights ob Moses to come an' moan an' de preacher to wrestle wid sin. De work ob de sperits an' de work ob de Lawd gwine jine han's tonight.

LIZE. I git's 'em, Auntie, from dey sleepin' beds. De Knights am a-comin'.

ANGELINE. Git on, den, git on de run. Time am runnin' low.
(LIZE *hurries off through the woods at the right.* AUNT ANGELINE *lifts her pot from the fire, walks slowly to the center of the clearing and places the pot on the ground. With her crooked stick raised, she makes the sign of the cross to the open sky, chanting softly, praying.*)

ANGELINE.

I makes de cross on de open do'.
Look down, Lawd, on de sin below.
I makes de cross on de do' ob de lamb—
Stretch yo' han' down, Lawd, wid a healin' ba'm.[1]

(*Turning to look up the hill, she raises her right arm, her fingers spread, and chants. Her tone is menacing, the rhythm faster.*)

1. Balm.

Come down, Plat Eye.
Shine in a stream.
Watch 'em, Plat Eye,
Wid de light ob green.
Fotch out de sin
To de beat ob de drum.
Send 'em 'way from de debil.
Make 'em come!

(*She picks up her pot and creeps off right through the woods, chanting.*)

Watch 'em, Plat Eye,
Make 'em 'fess de sin.
Watch 'em, Plat Eye,
Dey comin' in.
Watch 'em, watch 'em, watch 'em.

(*The sound of the* SINNERS *singing "Gwine Raise a Ruckus" as they come down the road drowns* ANGE-LINE'S *chanting.* SAPPORY *leads them in by the oak.* SAPPORY *is a slender girl of nineteen. Her crimson dress is molded to her body. Large gold loops swing from her ears. She is supported by* LOVIN' SAM, *a small "high yaller."* [1] *He wears a tan, checked suit, a yellow tie, and orange shoes. In his right hand he carries a portable victrola. It is evident that they have been drinking. They stagger down center.* RALINA *and* JOSHUA *follow.* RALINA *wears an old silk dress and a shapeless hat.* JOSHUA, *a big man, is dressed in old black pants, brown coat and a red tie.* BOOTCHIE *and* MOSE *come next.* BOOTCHIE, *small and very black, is sloppily dressed in a green blouse and red skirt.* MOSE *wears overalls.*

1. A Negro with a light-brown skin.

(COOT NAN *and* LINSON *struggle in wearily.* COOT NAN
*is simple-minded and agreeable, wearing a perpetual
grin. Her hair is plaited and wrapped with white
string. She wears a faded gingham dress.* LINSON *is fat
and lazy. He wears overalls. They flop down by the
big oak.* COOT NAN *sighs deeply.* LINSON *is stretched
out to his full length.*)

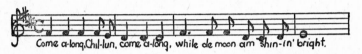

Come a-long, Chil-lun, come a-long, while de moon am shin-in' bright.

Git on boad,— down to town we go, Gwine raise a ru-ckus in dis night.

Come along, chillun, come along,
While de moon am shinin' bright.
Git on boa'd, down to town we go.
Gwine raise a ruckus [1] in dis night.

SAPPORY (*looking around the clearing*). Well, Lovin'
Sam, dis here our dance hall. Ain' no jazz band, ain'
no lights.

LOVIN' SAM. Don't need no jazz hall. Don' need no lights.
You gots what it takes to pleasure me wid.

BOOTCHIE (*watching jealously*). Listen to dat man sweet
talk. I bet he fix ebery 'oman he see.

MOSE (*quickly*). You min' yo' business, Bootchie.

LOVIN' SAM (*eloquently*). I chooses, madam. Miss Sappory is de queen ob all de wimmin I eber see.

1. A riotous party.

Bootchie (*disgustedly*). De queen, hunh?

Coot Nan (*rubbing her feet and sighing*). 'Fo' God, my feets done swol' up in a strut.

Ralina (*kicking off her shoes*). Ain't it de truf? Cain't wear shoes all day and not 'spec' yo' feets to swell. Shed dem shoes, Coot Nan. Here go mine.

Linson (*wearily*). 'Pears lak de wimmin am wore out wid raisin' de ruckus.

Joshua. Yeah, dey done give out. Sappory win de music box an' we sets here wid de dancin' goin' to waste.

Bootchie. What kind ob dice you roll, Sappory? You win dat music box powerful quick.

Sappory (*turning on her quickly*). De same kind as you roll, 'oman. You better min' how you talk.

Bootchie. I thinks you better min' how you sashays roun' here. You gots a life-breavin' husband what 'ull tend to you.

Sappory (*getting up quickly, she reaches in the top of her stocking, gets her folding razor, and threatens Bootchie with it*). You shet yo' mouf, Bootchie Nelson. When I needs you to he'p me hol' a man, I axes you to and not befo'.

Bootchie (*walking toward her, an open pocket knife in her hand*). Ain' nobody said nothin' 'bout holdin' a man. I gits de one I wants good as you can.

Ralina (*starting toward them*). Bofe y'all drunk, an' yellin' to wake de daid.

SAPPORY (*turning to* RALINA, *threatening her*). Drunk?
Who ain' drunk here? From de fu'st to de las', da's
what I axes you. Who ain' drunk?

RALINA (*pushing* SAPPORY *away from* BOOTCHIE). Oh,
my God A'mighty! We ain' wantin' no woman fight
here. Open up dat music box, Mr. Sam. Git to dancin',
peoples, git to dancin'.
(LOVIN' SAM *opens the music box.*)

JOSHUA. Play dem blues, dem city blues.

COOT NAN (*struggling to her feet*). Well, I kin make it
ef y'all kin. Git up, Linson. (*He does not move.*)
Move, nigger, you ain' 'sleep. (*She pulls him to his
feet.*)

LOVIN' SAM (*beginning to dance toward* SAPPORY *as the
music starts*). Come on, baby, shuffle dem shoes.

SAPPORY (*dancing to meet him*). I ready, man. Grab a
holt.
(SAPPORY *and* LOVIN' SAM *meet. They begin dancing
together.* MOSE *takes* BOOTCHIE, *flings her into his arms
and begins dancing as fast as the music will let him.*
RALINA *and* JOSHUA *dance a double shuffle.* COOT NAN
tries in vain to make LINSON *move faster. She breaks
away from him and, while he does a slow shuffle, she
dances around him.* LOVIN' SAM *and* SAPPORY, *being
fancy steppers, require more room than the others.*
LOVIN' SAM *slings* SAPPORY *halfway across the clearing. They dance alone, then writhe back together
again. As they dance close together, cheek to cheek,*
RALINA *screams.* SAPPORY *and* LOVIN' SAM *pay no at-*

tention and continue. The other SINNERS *stop still, watching.*)

RALINA (*screaming*). Look out, Sappory! Bill comin' at you.
(BILL, *a big black Negro, comes into the clearing from the right. A large butcher knife gleams in his hand. He stands for a moment watching the dance, then moves in a measured fury toward* SAPPORY *and* LOVIN' SAM. *Taking* SAPPORY *by the shoulder, he tears her away from* LOVIN' SAM, *stabs her in the shoulder, and throws her to the ground.* LOVIN' SAM *runs off through the woods towards the town.* JOSHUA *moves to stop the music.* COOT NAN *stands wide-mouthed.* RA-LINA *is terrified.* BOOTCHIE *looks half-pleased.*)

BILL (*looking at* SAPPORY *with disgust*). Maybe I fix her dis time. (*Turning quickly.*) Now where dat yellow-skin ape? I rip him open. (*He starts out after him.* MOSE *stops him.*)

MOSE. No, you ain', Bill. He running toward de white folks' yard. Don' mess after dat trash, Bill.

RALINA (*runs to* SAPPORY *and drops on her knees beside her*). Do, Jedus, Bill! You done slice her deep.
(*All the* SINNERS *except* BOOTCHIE *crowd around.*)

COOT NAN. Have mercy!

RALINA. Give me a rag, Coot Nan. Tear me a rag. Here, Bootchie, holp me wid de bleedin'.
(COOT NAN *stands dumb.* BOOTCHIE *keeps her distance.*)

BOOTCHIE (*sulkily*). I ain' messin' wid no fightin'. I ain' messin' wid it.

RALINA (*exasperated*). Well, stan' dere den. Jist stan' dere. Where de rag, Coot Nan?

COOT NAN (*tearing the skirt of her dress and handing a rag to* RALINA). Here. Take dis.

SAPPORY (*wailing*). You done cut de arm from de shoulder. You done cut de arm from de shoulder. De blood run red from de vein.

BILL (*looking down at her*). You shet up dat yelling, Sappory. You ain' kilt. You ought to be—
(BOOTCHIE, *curious, moves toward* SAPPORY. COOT NAN, *looking into the woods up right, steps back, terrified. Her mouth drops open. She sees a stream of green light coming from above the trees and falling directly upon the* SINNERS.)

COOT NAN. Look yonder, look yonder, peoples. What dat light? Look at dat light!
(*The* SINNERS *turn to see the light, which has grown stronger. Terrified, they move close together.*)

RALINA. Don' move. Don' move.

SAPPORY. Hit de Plat Eye watchin'. Hit de Plat Eye! I feels hit. (*Half sobbing.*) Bill, you done brought de Plat Eye on us.

BILL (*moving closer to* SAPPORY). I done brought him?

COOT NAN (*wildly*). Where we gwine hide?

LINSON. Dey ain' no hidin'.
(*The* SINNERS *fall on their knees, crouching close to-*

gether. *As they turn away, the steady monotonous beat of a drum comes throbbing through the darkness.*)

BOOTCHIE (*wailing*). Hit Aunt Angie! Hit Aunt Angie! Hear de drum a-startin'?
(*The slow haunting sound of* THE KNIGHTS OF MOSES *singing as they march through the woods sends a new terror through all the* SINNERS.)

SAPPORY. Oh, Jedus, Lawd! Dere Ma an' de Knights.

JOSHUA. Shet up. Shet up, all ob you.
(*Beating the ground with her stick,* ANGELINE *leads the procession through the woods. Behind her* THE KNIGHTS OF MOSES, *dressed in white praying robes and white headdresses, move slowly to the rhythm of the drum. Arms folded in front of them, heads held high, they make their slow march into the clearing, singing* "No Hidin' Place.")

Oh, dere's no hidin' place down here,
Oh, dere's no hidin' place down here,
Oh, I went to de rock to hide my face,
De rock cried out, "No hidin' place,"
Dere's no hidin' place down here.

(ANGELINE *stops in front of the crouching* SINNERS. THE KNIGHTS *stand behind her. In the exhortation which follows* ANGELINE *is the leader of the chanting and dancing. The movements which she suggests are taken up, strengthened, broadened, and made into a dance by* THE KNIGHTS OF MOSES. *The chants of* ANGELINE, THE KNIGHTS OF MOSES, *and the* SINNERS *blend together. There is no break between challenge and response. The tempo and volume gradually increase, building to a climax. The drumbeat continues throughout.*)

ANGELINE (*slowly*).

> Sinners, sinners, turn yo'se'f roun',
> Dey ain' no place to hide.

(*Pointing to the Plat Eye, she brings her arm down and leans over toward the cowering* SINNERS.)

> De light am on you,
> Fo' to see out yo' soul,
> Fo' to burn out de hell inside.

KNIGHTS OF MOSES (*right arms reaching to the left, they make a slow half-circle to right*).

> Burn out de hell, burn out de hell!

ANGELINE.

> Does you see hit shinin'?
> Feel it burn?

SINNERS.

>Sees hit shinin',
>Feels hit burn.

ANGELINE (*stronger*).

>Feel hit cut out your heart
>Lak' a cut-away worm.

SINNERS (*wailing*).

>Lak' a cut-away worm,

(*Slower.*)

>Lak' a cut-away worm.

(ANGELINE *emphasizes the rhythm strongly. Her
right arm raised high, three fingers spread to make a
fork, she brings her arm down toward them.*)

ANGELINE.

>Does you see de debil,
>Comin' down de light?
>Does you see de debil,
>Creepin' t'r'u' de night?
>Does you see de debil,
>Creepin' down,
>Wid a fork in he han'
>To turn you roun'?

KNIGHTS OF MOSES (*right arms raised over their heads,
their fingers spread, they walk slowly toward the
SINNERS*).

Wid a fork in he han',
Wid a fork in he han',
Wid a long red fork to roast you wid.

SINNERS (*shrinking, rocking back and forth*).

Oh, my Jedus! Oh, my Lawd!
Sabe us, Jedus! Sabe us, Lawd!

ANGELINE (*faster*).

Does you see de fires ob hell a-leapin',
Wid de sinners wailin' an' de sinners
weepin'?

KNIGHTS OF MOSES (*swaying from side to side, heads thrown back*).

Sinners wailin' an' de sinners weepin'.

ANGELINE (*her fingers spread and curved like flames, her right arm writhes across her body, pointing up right to the Plat Eye*).

Does you see de fires ob hell a-leapin'?
Does you see de fires?
Does you see 'em?

KNIGHTS OF MOSES (*following* ANGELINE'S *movement*).

See de fires! See de fires!

ANGELINE (*bringing her arm down, pointing to the* SINNERS).

Dere Plat Eye, burn 'em down.
Dey got sin in dey heart.
Dey got sin in dey soul.

KNIGHTS OF MOSES (*same movement as* ANGELINE).

Sin in dey heart,
Sin in dey soul.

ANGELINE (*pointing to* SAPPORY, *then to* BILL).

Fotch out Sappory, de sinful wife.
Fotch out Bill, fo' de slashin' knife.
Git on yo' feets, you cain't lay low.
Git on yo' feets, you gwine reap
   what you sow.

KNIGHTS OF MOSES (*arms reaching down to the* SINNERS,
palms up, they lift their arms slowly).

Gwine reap what you sow,
Gwine reap what you sow.

(BILL *and* SAPPORY *get to their feet slowly. They shrink back in terror. The* SINNERS, *rocking on their knees, keep up their wailing.*)

ANGELINE (*faster, with marked rhythm*).

> Does you see de sin you been libin' in?
> De deep, black sin you been libin' in?
> Does you see how de debil done lead you down,
> An' turn you roun', turn you roun'?

KNIGHTS OF MOSES (*threatening*).

> > De debil lead 'em,
> > De debil lead 'em.

ANGELINE.

> You done forsook de ways ob de Lawd.
> God gwine smite you fo' leabin' de Lawd.
> Does you see what you done, sinners all?
> Does you see what you done, how low you fall?

KNIGHTS OF MOSES.

> > Low you fall, low you fall.

ANGELINE.

> > De Lawd gwine smite you!
> > De Lawd gwine smite you!

(THE KNIGHTS OF MOSES *and* ANGELINE *bend to the left, right arms stretched across their bodies to the left. Their arms move to the right, cutting sharply back to the left.*)

KNIGHTS OF MOSES *and* ANGELINE.

> De Lawd gwine smite you.
> De Lawd gwine smite you.
> Gwine cut you down wid he fiery swo'd.

SINNERS (*rocking and swaying, begin beseeching slowly*).

> Oh, Jedus, Lawd,
> Lift dat swo'd,
> Lift dat swo'd,
> Lift dat swo'd.

(*They cry louder, rising on their knees with arms lifted.*)

> Oh, Jedus, Lawd,
> Lift dat swo'd.
> We heaby laden,
> Totin' de load.
> Lift dat swo'd,
> Lift dat swo'd.

ANGELINE.

> You moans lak sinners
> Wrastlin' wid sin.
> Is you ready now
> To 'fess de sin?

SINNERS.

> We ready, Jedus!
> We ready, Lawd!

(*The green light of the Plat Eye begins to grow dim.*)

KNIGHTS OF MOSES.

> Oh, moan it, moan it,
> Fo' de Lawd to hear,
> Pray out loud fo' de Lawd to hear.

SINNERS.

        Oh, Jedus, Lawd!

KNIGHTS OF MOSES.

        Moan it chile.

SINNERS.

        Oh, Jedus, Lawd!
        We been libin' wile.
        Sabe us, Jedus!
        Take de sin away.
        Sabe us, Jedus!
        Can't you hear us pray?

KNIGHTS OF MOSES *and* ANGELINE.

        Look down, Lawd!
        Dey moanin', moanin'.
        Look down, Lawd!
        Dey groanin', groanin'.

SINNERS.

        Jedus, Lawd!
        Hit's de fruit ob sin.
        We griebin', Lawd
        Wid de trouble we'se in.

(ANGELINE *turns up right, her right arm raised high and bathed in the dimming green light. Keeping the rhythm of the chant, she calls to the Lord. In answer to her cry the green light fades; and, as her arm descends, a soft, rosy light floods the clearing, falling on the* SINNERS *and* THE KNIGHTS OF MOSES.)

ANGELINE.

>Yes, my Lawd, send de heabenly sign.
>De heabenly sign,
>De heabenly sign!
>Yes, my Lawd, send de heabenly sign,
>To wash 'em in de blood ob de Lamb.

(*She pauses a moment as the light grows stronger. Looking up the hill, she calls into the darkness.*)

>I gives de sinners to de 'sciple ob de Lawd.
>Come out, brudder, from de darksome night.
>Show de sinners de way to de heabenly light.

(*The rich, powerful voice of* THE PREACHER *resounds through the darkness. He comes slowly down the hill into the light. The power of his presence gives silence to the* SINNERS.)

THE PREACHER.

>A charge to keep I have!
>A God to glorify!
>Confess to de Lawd de sin ob your ways,
>Prepare fo' heaben befo' you die.

(*About half-way down the hill* THE PREACHER *stops and stands looking down at the* SINNERS *and* THE KNIGHTS OF MOSES.)

>Is you sinners?

SINNERS.

>Sinners all.
>Sinners all.

THE PREACHER.

> Is you seen de debil
> An' de fires ob hell?

SINNERS.

> Seen de debil
> An' de fires ob hell.

SAPPORY (*falling to her knees*).

> Lawd, I seen 'em
> Leapin' high.
> Oh, Jedus, Lawd, don' pass me by.

THE PREACHER.

> Does you repent fo' your sinful ways?

SAPPORY.

> I repents, Oh Lawd, fo' de res' ob my days.

BILL (*falling to his knees*).

> Dis sorrow, Lawd, done bu'st my heart.
> I repents, my Lawd, I wants a new start.

THE PREACHER.

> All you sinners
> Min' how you lib.
> God am good an' He forgive.
> Come any more sinnin'
> Roun' dis place,
> God mos' likely
> Hide He Face.

SINNERS.

> No more sinnin'
> Roun' dis place.
> Gwine be no more sinnin'
> Roun' dis place.

(THE KNIGHTS OF MOSES *and the* SINNERS *fall to their knees moaning softly throughout the prayer.*)

THE PREACHER.

> Oh, Lawd, dey wrastle
> Wid sin t'r'u' de night.
> Oh, Lawd, dey humble
> In de mawnin' light.

KNIGHTS OF MOSES.

> Amen, Lawd, Amen.

THE PREACHER.

> Oh, Lawd, forgib' 'em.
> Dey sin is tol'.

SINNERS.

> Hear us, Jedus.

PREACHER.

> Oh, Lawd, forgib' 'em.
> Take 'em back in de fol'.

SINNERS.

> Oh, Lawd, forgib' us.
> Oh, Lawd, forgib' us.

THE PREACHER.

> Amen. Amen.

(*The morning light now fills the sky. The road up the hill can be seen clearly. Mount Zion on its crest stands above them, friendly and protecting. The* SINNERS *rise slowly to their feet.* THE KNIGHTS OF MOSES *lift their arms.* ANGELINE *points toward the open sky. She is transfigured. Her voice is soft and high.*)

ANGELINE.

> Dere de light ob de mawnin' sun
> Rise to bring de day.
> De Lawd from glory sent de fiery ball
> To wash de night away.
> Can you hear de angels
> Singin' roun' de throne,
> An' God watchin' sinners
> Marchin' home?

KNIGHTS OF MOSES *and* SINNERS (*softly*).

> Hear de angels.

(THE PREACHER *lifts the song* "One Mawnin' Soon." *Almost immediately the* SINNERS *and* THE KNIGHTS OF MOSES *take it up.*)

One mawnin' soon, one mawnin' soon, My Lawd,
One mawnin' soon, I hearn de angels singin'.
All roun' my room, all round' my room, My Lawd,
All roun' my room, I hearn de angels singin'.

(*As the song builds up,* THE KNIGHTS OF MOSES, *with their arms raised high, turn slowly around; and, as the song dies away, they are again facing* THE PREACHER. *He raises his head, the glory shining on his face, and shouts:*)

THE PREACHER.

> Yeah, Yeah!
> I can see it in my min'.
> De heaben open up
> An' de glory shine!
> De angels a-playin'
> On de harp of gold.
> And de Christians a-shoutin',
> Lawd, sabe my soul!

KNIGHTS OF MOSES *and* SINNERS (*shouting, rocking, beating their feet with the rhythm*).

> Hallelujah, de glory shine.
> De glory shine fo' de Lawd.
> De angel playin' on de harp ob gol'!
> An' we'se a-shoutin',
> Lawd, sabe my soul!

THE PREACHER (*his arms raised over the* SINNERS *ana* THE KNIGHTS OF MOSES).

> De mercy ob de Lawd
> Am a healin' ba'm!
> He hab' washed us in de blood
> Ob de Lamb!

(ANGELINE *shakes hands with* THE PREACHER. *With the ecstasy and the fervor of the redeemed they all sing "Washed in de Blood."* THE PREACHER *and* ANGE-

LINE *walk slowly up the hill.* THE KNIGHTS OF MOSES,
*filled with joy, follow, waving their arms. "De sperit"
is upon them and their bodies jerk and sway to the
syncopated rhythm of the song. In a frenzy of exalta-
tion the* SINNERS *shout and writhe, accenting the
rhythm with the beat of their feet.* SAPPORY, *completely filled with "de sperit," dances in front of the*
SINNERS, *shouting "Hallelujah!" until she falls exhausted against* BILL, *who supports her.* BILL *and* SAP-
PORY *lead the rest of the* SINNERS *up the hill, their
faces shining in the glory of the morning light.)*

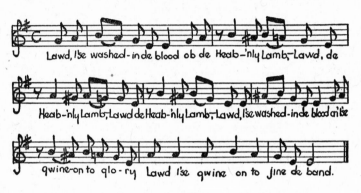

Lawd, I'se washed in de blood
Ob de heabenly Lamb, Lawd, de heabenly Lamb, Lawd,
De heabenly Lamb, Lawd.
I'se washed in de blood,
An' I'se gwine on to glory, Lawd,
I'se gwine on to jine de band.
Oh, I libed in de sin ob de yearth below, Lawd,
De yearth below, Lawd, de yearth below, Lawd.
Den I hearn de cry, "Sinner, rise an' go,"
Lawd, I'se gwine on to jine de band.

CURTAIN